DEVELOPING POTENTIAL ACROSS
A FULL RANGE OF LEADERSHIP™

Cases on Transactional
and Transformational Leadership

DEVELOPING POTENTIAL ACROSS A FULL RANGE OF LEADERSHIP™

Cases on Transactional and Transformational Leadership

Edited by

Bruce J. Avolio
Bernard M. Bass
Center for Leadership Studies
School of Management
SUNY–Binghamton

LEA LAWRENCE ERLBAUM ASSOCIATES, PUBLISHERS
2002 Mahwah, New Jersey London

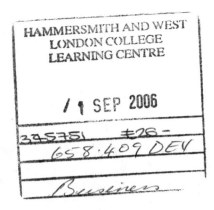
Lawrence Erlbaum Associates, Inc., Publishers
10 Industrial Avenue
Mahwah, New Jersey 07430

Cover design by Kathryn Houghtaling-Lacey

Library of Congress Cataloging-in-Publication Data

Developing potential across a full range of leaderships : Cases on transactional and
transformational leadership / Bruce J. Avolio and Bernard M. Bass.
  p.   cm.
Includes bibliographical references and indexes.
ISBN 0-8058-3894-5 (pbk. : alk. paper)
1. Leadership—Case studies. I. Avolio, Bruce J. II. Bass, Bernard M.
HD57.7 .D498 2002
658.4′092—dc21

2001-033043
CIP

Books published by Lawrence Erlbaum Associates are printed on acid-free paper,
and their bindings are chosen for strength and durability.

Printed in the United States of America
10 9 8 7 6 5 4 3 2

Contents

Preface   vii

Introduction   1

I ATTITUDES AND BEHAVIOR OF INDIVIDUAL LEADERS

1 Still Flying High After All These Years at Southwest Airlines   13

2 Colin Powell's Thoughts on Leadership   16

3 In the Land of Cornflakes and Car Assembly   20

4 Can You Name America's Seven Best Bosses?   24

5 Leading by Listening   36

6 Patricia Gallup, CEO, PC Connection (Excerpts)   42

7 Global Leadership   48

8 Turnaround Drama Instills Leadership   55

9 Leading Ladies   62

10 The Many Facets of Tina's Leadership   66

II LEADER DEVELOPMENT AND SUCCESSION

11 Playing Powell Politics 73

12 Larry Bossidy 76

13 Gertrude Boyle 79

14 A. Diane Moeller: A Talk With the Healthcare Forum's
Incoming Chair 84

15 Leadership of Renewal: Leadership for the 21st Century 88

16 Profiles of Two Successful Women Managers 96

17 Nimrod Press 98

III STRATEGIES AND THEIR IMPLEMENTATION

18 The Future at Telview 111

19 David Glassman: Division Manager in Telview 116

20 Joan Rivers' Memo 125

21 Back to the Past When the Future Seemed So Obvious 130

22 Amy's Debrief 134

23 A Doll's House 138

IV ETHICAL ISSUES

24 Managerial Ethical Leadership: Adrian Cadbury 149

25 Jim Corby 152

26 The Commandant's Dilemma 154

27 Jack Gets a Grip 159

28 The Fine Art of Leadership 164

Preface

This is a volume of 28 cases. In each case, the focus is on the leadership style of the key players. The cases were chosen to present all facets of a model of leadership, which says that the most effective leaders are *both* transformational and transactional in their leadership style. Cases were selected for inclusion and/or developed to provide examples of leaders from across the spectrum of public and private sectors. Specific emphasis was placed on selecting male and female leaders from a broad array of cultures.

Purpose of This Book. A great deal has been written about a model of leadership that we refer to as a "full range" of leadership potential. This book adds to the literature, by highlighting specific people who exemplify the various styles and orientations regarding a full range of leadership potential.

Intended Audience. We expect that practitioners who conduct or facilitate leadership training will find this book quite useful to their work. In addition, managers interested in developing their own leadership potential will be able to learn by example how different styles affect leadership performance. This book can also be used as a supplement to other books on leadership for undergraduate, graduate, and executive education courses in management.

Transformational leaders tend to be:

Idealized and inspiring: They act as role models; take calculated risks; demonstrate high standards of ethical conduct; and are admired, respected, and trusted by their followers. Such leaders provide meaning and challenge. They arouse team spirit, envision attractive futures, and demonstrate a clear sense of purpose and commitment to the mission.

Intellectually stimulating: They frame and reframe problems, question assumptions, and stimulate followers and peers to creative thinking and innovation.

Individually considerate: They show concern for the well-being of each person they work with, and treat each as an individual with unique needs and capabilities. They place a considerable amount of attention on developing each person to his or her full potential.

Transactional leaders tend to be:

Contingently rewarding: They provide rewards and/or promises for people who meet standards of performance set jointly or by the leader.

Active in managing by exception: They monitor followers' performance and take corrective action as needed.

Nontransactional passive leaders wait for problems to arise before taking action, avoid making decisions, or are not around when needed.

Each leader has a profile that includes some or all of these transformational, transactional, and nontransactional behaviors. The better leaders do both, and the best leaders are more transformational than transactional.

In the first 27 cases, you will find one or more components of a full range of leadership illustrated for discussion. Some of the leaders profiled exhibit certain components of leadership to a much greater extent than they do other components.

Case 28 illustrates a false leadership. The leaders discussed seem like transformational leaders but think and act in ways to benefit only themselves at the expense of others—they are pseudotransformational and pseudotransactional leaders.

Discussion of the cases highlights how to build balance in one's leadership profile to optimize the potential of leaders, followers, and their organizations. The presence or absence of styles in a wide variety of contexts is discussed in terms of the effects on individuals, groups, or organizations. Discussion questions are posed at the end of each case. The book begins with an overview of what constitutes transactional and transformational leadership. This discussion is then expanded to include what we term a *full range of leadership potential*™.

We wish to acknowledge Juliette Monet and Ben Laurenzi for their assistance in helping identify the cases that were ultimately selected; Wendy Kramer, who helped put all the pieces together; and Sally Bowers, Bernadette Cencetti, and Maureen Whitney for their data-processing assistance.

—Bruce J. Avolio
—Bernard M. Bass
Binghamton, New York

Introduction

Transformational leaders motivate others to do more than they originally intended and often even more than they thought possible. Such leaders set more challenging expectations and typically achieve higher performances. Transformational leadership is an expansion of transactional leadership. Transactional leadership emphasizes the transaction or exchange that takes place among leaders, colleagues, and followers. This exchange is based on the leader discussing with others what is required and specifying the conditions and rewards these others will receive if they fulfill the requirements. True transformational leaders raise the level of moral maturity of those whom they lead. They convert their followers into leaders. They broaden and enlarge the interests of those whom they lead. They motivate their associates, colleagues, followers, clients, and even their bosses to go beyond their individual self-interests for the good of the group, organization, or society. Transformational leaders address each follower's sense of self-worth in order to engage the follower in true commitment and involvement in the effort at hand. This is one of the things that transformational leadership adds to the transactional exchange (Shamir, 1991).

Since the 1980s, research has supported the idea that transformational leadership is more effective than transactional leadership in generating the extra effort, commitment, and satisfaction of those led. Constructive transactional leadership or contingent reward is reasonably effective under most circumstances. Management by exception is more corrective than constructive. But actively correcting a follower for failure to perform as expected is more varied in effects. Corrective leadership that is passive (don't fix it if it ain't broken) tends to be ineffective (Levinson, 1980). Laissez-faire leaders avoid their responsibilities to lead.

COMPONENTS OF TRANSFORMATIONAL LEADERSHIP

Transformational leaders do more with colleagues and followers than set up simple exchanges or agreements. They behave in ways to achieve superior results by employing one or more of the four components of transformational leadership. First, leadership is idealized when followers seek to identify with their leaders and emulate them. Second, the leadership inspires the followers with challenge and persuasion that provide meaning and understanding. Third, the leadership is intellectually stimulating, expanding the followers use of their abilities. Finally, the leadership is individually considerate, providing the followers with support, mentoring, and coaching. Each of these components can be assessed with the Multifactor Leadership Questionnaire (MLQ). In the questionnaire, you can describe yourself as a leader. Those who work for you, with you, and for whom you work can do the same assessment of you.

Idealized Leadership. Transformational leaders behave in ways that make them role models for their followers. Such leaders are admired, respected, and trusted. Followers identify with these leaders and want to emulate them. Among the things the leader does to earn this credit is consider the needs of others over his or her own personal needs. The leader shares risks with followers and is consistent rather than arbitrary. He or she can be counted on to do the right thing, demonstrating high standards of ethical and moral conduct. He or she avoids using power for personal gain and in fact uses his or her power only when needed.

Inspirational Motivation. Transformational leaders behave in ways that motivate and inspire those around them by providing meaning and challenge to their followers' work. Team spirit is aroused. Enthusiasm and optimism are displayed. The leader gets followers involved in envisioning attractive future states. The leader clearly communicates expectations that followers want to meet, and demonstrates commitment to goals and the shared vision.

Intellectual Stimulation. Transformational leaders stimulate their followers' efforts to be innovative and creative by questioning assumptions, reframing problems, and approaching old situations in new ways. Creativity is encouraged. There is no public criticism of individual members' mistakes. New ideas and creative problem solutions are solicited from followers, who are included in the process of addressing problems and finding solutions. Followers are encouraged to try new approaches, and their ideas are not criticized if they differ from the leader's ideas.

Individualized Consideration. Transformational leaders pay special attention to each individual's needs for achievement and growth by acting as a coach or mentor. Followers and colleagues are developed to successively higher levels of potential. Individualized consideration is practiced as follows: New learning opportunities are created along with a supportive climate. Individual differences in terms of needs and desires are recognized. The leader's behavior demonstrates acceptance of individual differences (e.g., some employees receive more encouragement, some more autonomy, others firmer standards, and still others more task structure). A two-way exchange in communication is encouraged, and "management by walking around" is practiced. Interactions with followers are personalized (e.g., the leader remembers previous conversations, is aware of individual concerns, and sees the individual as a whole person rather than as just an employee). The individually considerate leader listens effectively. The leader delegates tasks as a means of developing followers. Delegated tasks are monitored to see if the followers need additional direction or support and to assess progress; ideally, followers do not feel they are being checked up on.

Several thousand leaders in the private sector and community leaders in the public sector have been trained using the model of the *full range of leadership*. This model includes the four components of transformational leadership, as well as transactional leadership behavior and laissez-faire or nonleadership behavior.

COMPONENTS OF TRANSACTIONAL LEADERSHIP

Transactional leadership occurs when the leader rewards or disciplines a follower depending on the adequacy of the follower's performance. Transactional leadership depends on contingent reinforcement, either positive contingent reward or the more negative active or passive forms of management-by-exception.

Contingent Reward. This constructive transaction has been found to be reasonably effective, although not as much as any of the transformational components in motivating others to achieve higher levels of development and performance. With this method, the leader assigns or gets agreement on what needs to be done, and promises rewards or actually rewards others in exchange for satisfactorily carrying out the assignment.

Management by Exception. This corrective transaction tends to be more ineffective, but it may be required in certain situations. Management by exception may be active or passive. When active, the leader arranges to actively monitor deviances from standards, mistakes, and errors in the follower's assignments and to take corrective action as necessary. When passive, the leader waits for deviances, mistakes, and errors to occur and then takes corrective action.

Laissez-Faire Leadership. This is the avoidance or absence of leadership. It is, by definition, the most inactive form of leadership. As well, it is the most ineffective, according to almost all research on the style. Under laissez-faire leadership, nothing is transacted.

Fundamental to the full-range leadership model is the fact every leader displays each style to some extent. An optimal profile is shown in Fig. 1B. The third dimension of this model (depth) represents how frequently a leader displays a particular style of leadership. The active dimension is by self-evident definition; the effectiveness dimension is based on the results of many research studies.

In Fig. I.1, the leader infrequently displays laissez-faire (LF) leadership, higher frequencies of the transactional leadership styles of passive (MBE-P) and active managing by exception (MBE-A), and more contingent reward or constructive transaction (CT), and most of the transformational components (the 4 Is—idealistic influence, inspiration, intelligent stimulation, and

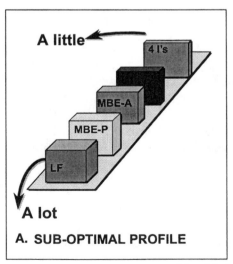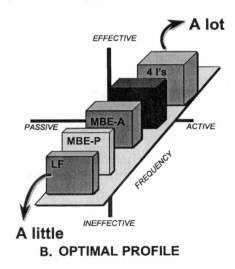

FIG. I.1. Contrasting full range leadership profiles (individual level).

individualized consideration). In contrast, as shown in Fig. I.1A, the poorly performing leader tends toward more laissez-faire leadership (LF), active managing by exception (MBE-A), passive management by exception (MBE-P), and less transformational leadership of the 4 Is.

Many research studies of the models shown in Fig. I.1 have been conducted in business and industry, government, the military, educational institutions, and nonprofit organizations, all showing that transformational leaders, as measured by the MLQ survey instruments derived from the Avolio and Bass model, were more effective and satisfying as leaders than were transactional leaders, although the best leaders frequently employ some of the latter but more of the former. Follow-up investigations have shown that developing transformational leadership with training in its four components can enhance a leader's effectiveness and satisfaction. Other findings included:

- Executives in 28 different organizations who championed projects displayed more transformational behaviors than did 28 matched non-champions (Howell & Higgins, 1990).
- Transformational leadership was higher among innovative school principals (Leithwood & Steinbach, 1991) than among noninnovative school principals.
- Transformational leadership was higher among Marine Corps commanders of more highly effective helicopter squadrons (Salter, 1989) than those of less effective squadrons.
- Transformational leadership was higher among those Methodist ministers with greater Sunday church attendance and membership growth (Onnen, 1987) than among other Methodist ministers.
- Transformational leadership was higher among presidents of MBA teams completing complex simulations with greater financial success than among their peers (Avolio, Waldman, & Einstein, 1988). Transformational leadership was also high among business managers whose departments eventually achieved future financial success (Howell & Avolio, 1993).
- Managers who were seen as transformational by their followers earned better performance evaluations from committees of their superiors (Hater & Bass, 1988) than did those not viewed as transformational.
- Naval officers who were rated as more transformational by their subordinates earned from their superiors both recommendations for early promotion and better fitness reports than did those officers rated as less transformational (Yammarino & Bass, 1990).

Among the components of transformational leadership, idealized influence and inspirational leadership are most effective and satisfying; individualized consideration is a bit less so. But in turn, all four Is of transformational leadership are more effective than is constructive transaction. However, constructive transactions remain reasonably effective and satisfying in most situations, except where a leader has no control of the ways a follower may be rewarded for good performance. Actively taking corrective action—that is, managing by exception by arranging to monitor the performance of followers—is somewhat less effective and satisfying, but passively waiting for problems to arise or remaining oblivious until a mishap occurs is seen as poor, ineffective leadership and is dissatisfying. The most ineffective and dissatisfying style is laissez-faire leadership—avoiding leadership and abdicating responsibilities. Analyses of over 5,000 cases have affirmed these findings (Lowe, Kroeck, & Sivasubramaniam, 1996).

Transformational leadership adds to transactional leadership in its effects on follower satisfaction and performance. Transformational leadership does not replace transactional leadership. That is, constructive and especially corrective transactions may have only marginal impact on followers unless accompanied by one or more components of transformational leadership for getting the most out of transactions: The follower needs to feel valued by the leader, the follower needs to find meaning in what he or she is doing, and the follower needs a sense of ownership in what's being done.

Transactional leadership, particularly contingent reward, provides a broad basis for effective leadership, but a greater amount of effort, effectiveness, innovation, risk taking, and satisfaction can be achieved by transactional leadership if it is augmented by transformational leadership.

Transformational leadership can be directive or participative, as well as democratic or authoritarian, elitist or leveling. Sometimes, transformational leadership is misunderstood as elitist and antidemocratic. Since the 1930s, the praises of democratic, participative leadership have been sung. Most managers have at least learned that before making a decision it pays to consult with those who will implement the decision, although fewer managers pursue a democratic vote or strive for consensus in a participative discussion with all those involved. There are many good reasons for encouraging shared decision making, empowering followers, and self-managing. Nonetheless, many circumstances call for a leader to be authoritative, decisive, and directive. Democratic decisions can become a pooling of ignorance among a group of novices. Novices may wish direction and advice on what to do and how to do it. Even when no leader is appointed, someone must begin to take initiatives and soon comes to be seen as a leader. Many confuse transformational leadership with democratic, participative leadership. It often may be so, but at times it can also be directive, decisive, and authoritative. Idealized leaders can direct followers who are counting on them to help get the team out of a crisis by employing radical solutions to deal with the problems. Again, inspirational leaders can be highly directive in their appeals. Intellectually stimulating leaders may challenge their followers. Individually considerate leaders could rise above the demands for equality from their followers to treat them differently according to their different needs for growth.

At the same time, transformational leaders can share vision building and idea generation that could be a democratic and collective enterprise. Such leaders can encourage follower participation in the change processes involved. In the same way, transactional leadership can be either directive or participative.

Most leaders' profiles include both transformational and transactional leadership. The attitudes and behavior of Otto Von Bismarck, whose efforts led to the unification of Germany in 1871, illustrate how transformational and transactional leadership can be directive or participative, democratic or authoritative (Avolio & Bass, 1991).

Interviews with executives about the leadership they had seen produced numerous behavioral examples of transformational leadership. Idealized influence or charismatic leadership was attributed to the interviewees' leaders for demonstrating such traits as setting examples, showing determination, possessing extraordinary talents, taking risks, creating in followers a sense of empowerment, showing dedication to "the cause," creating a sense of a joint mission, dealing with crises using radical solutions, and engendering in their followers faith in the leadership. Inspirational leadership included providing meaning and challenge, painting an optimistic future, molding expectations, creating self-fulfilling prophesies, and thinking ahead. Intellectual stimulation was judged to be present when leaders questioned assumptions, encouraged followers to employ intuition, entertained ideas that may have seemed silly at first, created imaginative visions, asked subordinates to rework problems they thought had already been solved, and saw unusual patterns. Individualized consideration was apparent to interviewees when their leaders answered them with minimum delay, showed that they were concerned for their followers' well-being, assigned tasks based on needs and abilities, encouraged two-way exchanges of ideas, were available when needed, encouraged self-development, practiced walk-around management, and effectively mentored, counseled, and coached.

When peers of military cadet leaders were asked what characterized the important traits of a good leader, they tended to describe such traits of inspiration, intellectual stimulation, and individualized consideration as self-confidence, persuasiveness, concern for the well-being of others, the ability to articulate one's ideas and thoughts, providing models to be emulated by others, holding high expectations for him- or herself and others, keeping others well-informed, and maintaining high self-motivation (Atwater, Lau, Bass, Avolio, Camobreco, & Whitmore, 1994).

The Full Range of Leadership Development Program (Avolio & Bass, 1991) begins with participants describing their implicit theories of leadership as evidenced by an ideal leader each has known. Invariably, for well over 5,000 trainees, the characteristics of the ideal leader have included the four components of transformational and transactional contingent reward leadership.

PSEUDO LEADERS

So far, we have only presented the transformational leader who works for the good of other individuals, the group, the community, or society. We now must take note of the *pseudotransformational leader*. Transformational leadership may be socialized or personalized. Socialized leadership is based on egalitarian behavior, serves collective interests, and develops and empowers others. Socialized leaders tend to be altruistic and to use legitimate established channels of authority (Howell & House, 1992; McClelland, 1975). Eleanor Roosevelt was the epitome of socialized leadership. Personalized leadership is based on personal dominance and authoritarian behavior, is self-aggrandizing, serves the self-interest, and is exploitative of others (McClelland, 1975). Personalized leaders rely heavily on manipulation, threat, and punishment, and show disregard for both the established institutional procedures and for the rights and the feelings of others. They are impulsively aggressive, narcissistic, and impetuous (Howell & House, 1992). Adolf Hitler and Joseph Stalin were such leaders.

The dynamics of transformational leadership may look the same whether beneficial or harmful to followers (Bass, 1985), but the truly transformational leader is socialized in orientation and values as well as morally uplifting. By contrast, the pseudotransformational leader is personalized in orientation and values, and caters in the long run to his or her self-interests. Generally, such leaders leave behind a legacy of destruction, as opposed to a stronger community to build future success.

Truly transformational leaders transcend their own self-interests for one of two reasons: utilitarian or moral principles. If utilitarian, their objective is to (a) benefit the organization, society, the group, the attachment to the social group of which one is a member, the collective of individual members, and/or (b) to meet the challenges of the task or mission. If a matter of moral principles, the objective is to do the right thing—to do what fits principles of morality, responsibility, sense of discipline, and/or respect for authority, customs, rules, and traditions of a society. There is belief in the social responsibility of the leader and the organization. Tom Paine's writings illustrate the truly transforming leader in his appeals to reason in *Common Sense* and *Age of Reason*, appeals to principle in his *Rights of Man*, and his oft-quoted need for transcendence, "These are the times that try men's souls."

Pseudotransformational leaders are self-oriented, self-aggrandizing, exploitative, and narcissistic. Power-oriented pseudotransformational leaders openly preach distorted utilitarian and crooked moral principles. Both Hitler and Stalin enslaved and murdered millions whom they declared to be enemies of the state. The labor provided was cheap, and both leaders regarded the imprisonments and deaths as deserved.

Pseudotransactional leadership behavior can also be readily observed. A leader who promises rewards but does not deliver, a leader who monitors followers but fails to take corrective action, a leader who as problems arise points to organizational rules but actually invents them, or a leader who says nothing when an error occurs but calls attention to it after it is too late to do something about it—these are all classic examples of pseudotransactional leaders.

This book of cases will provide you with examples of people in leadership roles to help you understand the types of behaviors and actions that constitute a full range model of leadership and its development. The contents include:

- Cases of leaders we have either worked with or of whom we became aware.
- Cases of more prominent or famous people who demonstrated one or more of the leadership orientations along a full range of leadership potential.

Each case may be reviewed to identify actions or behaviors that represent one or more styles or perspectives of Full Range Leadership™. Questions are posed at the end of each case.

Actions taken in the case can be discussed from the following perspectives and questions:

- How does it affect your thinking about leading others? What was positive? What was negative?
- How would you feel if you were a follower (peer) in the case, or the recipient of leadership?
- How would you change what was done?
- What do you believe will be the long- and/or short-term impact of the actions taken?

- Can you provide an example of a leader who took similar actions? What were the long- and/or short-term impact and consequences?

The specific questions provided at the end of each case can be considered.

REFERENCES

Atwater, L. E., Lau, A. W., Bass, B. M., Avolio, B. J., Camobreco, J., & Whitmore, N. (1994). *The content, construct and criterion-related validity of leader behavior measures* (ARI Research Note 95-01). Alexandria, VA: U.S. Army Research Institute for the Behavioral and Social Sciences.

Avolio, B. J., & Bass, B. M. (1991). *The full range of leadership development: Basic and advanced manuals*. Binghamton, NY: Bass, Avolio & Associates.

Avolio, B. J., Waldman, D. A., & Einstein, W. O. (1988). Transformational leadership in a management simulation: Impacting the bottomline. *Group and Organization Studies, 13,* 59–80.

Bass, B. M. (1985). *Leadership and performance beyond expectations*. New York: Free Press.

Hater, J. J., & Bass, B. M. (1988). Superiors' evaluations and subordinates' perceptions of transformational and transactional leadership. *Journal of Applied Psychology, 73,* 695–702.

Howell, J. M., & Avolio, B. J. (1993). Transformational leadership, transactional leadership, locus of control, and support for innovation: Key predictors of consolidated business-unit performance. *Journal of Applied Psychology, 78,* 891–902.

Howell, J. M., & Higgins, C. A. (1990). Champions of technological innovations. *Administrative Science Quarterly, 35,* 317–341.

Howell, J. M., & House, R. J. (1992). *Socialized and personalized charisma: An essay on the bright and dark sides of leadership*. Unpublished manuscript, Western Business School, The University of Western Ontario, London, Ontario, Canada.

Leithwood, K., & Steinbach, R. (1991). Indicators of transformational leadership in everyday problem solving of school administrators. *Journal of Personnel Evaluation in Education, 4,* 221–243.

Levinson, H. (1980). Power, leadership and the management of stress. *Professional Psychology, 11,* 497–508.

Lowe, K., Kroeck, K. G., & Sivasubramaniam, N. (1996). Effectiveness correlates of transformational and transactional leadership: A meta-analytic review. *Leadership Quarterly, 7,* 385–425.

McClelland, D. C. (1975). *Power: The inner experience*. New York: Irvington.

Onnen, M. K. (1987). *The relationship of clergy and leadership characteristics to growing or declining churches*. Doctoral dissertation, University of Louisville, KY.

Salter, D. J. (1989). *Leadership styles in United States Marine Corps transport helicopter squadrons*. Master's thesis, Naval Postgraduate School, Monterey, CA.

Shamir, B. (1991). Meaning, self and motivation in organizations. *Organization Studies, 12,* 405–424.

Yammarino, F. J., & Bass, B. M. (1990). Long-term forecasting of transformational leadership and its effects among Naval officers: Some preliminary findings. In K. E. Clark & M. R. Clark (Eds.), *Measures of leadership* (pp. 151–184). West Orange, NJ: Leadership Library of America.

I

ATTITUDES AND BEHAVIOR OF INDIVIDUAL LEADERS

Although there are many similarities among successful and effective leaders, there are also wide differences in attitudes, beliefs, and behavior. Successful leaders get their followers to follow them; effective leaders motivate and enable their followers to reach shared goals. Such leaders create a sense of alignment and direction that is shared by colleagues and followers.

See if you can determine what attitudes and behavior made for successful and effective leaders in the first nine cases. Read Part I looking for the attitudes, actions, and behavior that characterize successful and effective leaders. Try to examine the leadership of these individuals as if you were a follower. The cases in Part I are as follows:

1. Still Flying High After All These Years at Southwest Airlines
2. Colin Powell's Thoughts on Leadership
3. In the Land of Cornflakes and Car Assembly
4. Can You Name America's Seven Best Bosses?
5. Leading by Listening
6. Patricia Gallup, CEO, PC Connection (Excerpts)
7. Global Leadership
8. Turnaround Drama Instills Leadership
9. Leading Ladies
10. The Many Facets of Tina's Leadership

CHAPTER

1

Still Flying High After All These Years
at Southwest Airlines*

Over the past 20 years, Southwest Airlines has shown the best results in the U.S. airline industry. Their success may be attributed to several things. The CEO and founder Herb Kelleher has placed emphasis on humor in the organization. He would like to build relationships with passengers and give them "an experience." The business strategy is based on simplicity, efficiency, and effectiveness. Employees are helpful to one another. Most important is the CEO's commitment to maintaining a quality workforce.

Although other airlines report record profits, the obvious question is what is so different about this airline versus all the rest, who limped through the 1980s barely surviving, if in fact they did survive. The big airlines like Eastern that were far better positioned to take advantage of the deregulation mania in the 1980s and early 1990s found themselves out of business, whereas little old Southwest chugged along toward increasing levels of profitability.

Some may attribute Southwest's success to its dynamic CEO and founder Herb Kelleher, who has been honored as the most admired CEO in the USA by his employees. Herb would attribute it to other factors, such as the people who work for Southwest Airlines. Both seem to admire each other, as evidenced perhaps by Southwest Airlines' turnover rate, which is the lowest in the U.S. airline industry.

When Southwest first began operations, Kelleher established several basic tenets to run the business. First, he focused on building relationships

*An original case written by the editors.

with customers and making flying "an experience." Southwest was one of the first companies in the world to highlight the importance of having a sense of humor in terms of developing its customer relationships. Similar to Ben and Jerry's ice cream company and Sun Microsystems, humor was considered a key corporate value, and in fact was measured as one of the core components in Southwest Airlines' job interviews. For example, Southwest is one of the few airlines where a flight attendant will sing the preflight instructions as a rap song. They also have a CEO who recently settled a large legal suit with a competitor by challenging the other CEO to arm wrestle with a winner-take-all outcome. Herb lost, but as he said at the arm wrestling event, so did all of the lawyers!

A second component of the business strategy is to keep things simple. All Southwest pilots currently fly 737s. With this strategy, they are able to cut maintenance and training expenses. Also, there are only a few job classifications and everyone is expected to join in and help each other to keep the planes flying. The sole restriction is that only the pilot is allowed to fly the plane, at least most of the time.

Related to simplicity, Southwest Airlines uses a very simple ticketing and reservation system. There are no frills. Also, due to the lack of boundaries in the company regarding this being "your" job versus "mine," Southwest is able to turn planes around 25% faster than competitors, thus keeping more planes in the air at any point in time. There are more planes in the air at less cost. Southwest achieves high levels of efficiency because all employees are willing to help clean the planes to get them off the gate, even Herb Kelleher, who often can be found down with the maintenance crew cleaning planes, and/or helping the baggage handlers.

Herb initially defined Southwest Airlines as being a competitor with buses, trains, and cars instead of other airlines. Specifically, he wanted it to be cheaper to fly Southwest than it would be to drive or take public transportation. Consequently, the choice becomes a "no brainer" for the customer. Would you rather drive 500 miles or take a plane in less time and for less money?

Finally, and perhaps one of the more important components in retaining a high-quality workforce, is the intense commitment that this CEO continually demonstrates to people. He frequently becomes involved in helping out employees personally. He reaches down and gets to know the people who work in his company, so they will understand what he truly values and believes in. And when asked what he feels toward his employees, he said, "I really love these people." He didn't say *like, respect, trust, care,* and so forth, he said he *loved them.* And for most people working for his airline, they seem to believe what Herb said is true, because they apparently love him too.

Discussion Questions

1. What aspects of this CEO's style relate to the full range of leadership model?
2. How does his style affect the culture of this organization?
3. Do you see any problems with what will happen to Southwest after Herb retires?
4. How can we take what Herb does well and apply it to expanding your full range of leadership potential?
5. If you were one of Herb's followers, how would you describe Herb to a prospective employee?

2

Colin Powell's Thoughts on Leadership*

As part of IndustryWeek's *(IW) series on the world's 100 best managed companies, Secretary of State General Colin L. Powell, at that time former Chairman of the Joint Chiefs of Staff and White House national security advisor, was asked about his views on leadership. According to Powell, leadership in the 21st century will not be much different from the leadership shown by Thomas Jefferson, George Washington, and their colleagues 200 years ago. Leadership will always require people who have a vision and the ability to motivate others.*

Perhaps no one in the U.S. is more respected for his views on leadership than Gen. Colin L. Powell, USA (Ret.), former Chairman of the Joint Chiefs of Staff, White House national security advisor, Secretary of State, and much-courted (he kept saying "no" in the 2000 election) candidate for President or Vice President. Author of the best-selling *My American Journey* (1995, Random House) Powell recently shared his views on leadership in this excerpted interview with IW.

IW: Will skills required by effective leaders in the 21st century differ from those of the 20th century?

Powell: I don't know that leadership in the 21st century will be essentially different from the leadership shown by Thomas Jefferson, George Washington, and their colleagues 200 years ago. Leadership will always require people who have a vision of where they

*Anonymous (1996, August 19). Colin Powell's thoughts on leadership. *Industry Week*, *245*(15), pp. 56–57. (Adapted)

wish to take "the led." Leadership will always require people who are able to organize the effort of [others] to accomplish the objectives that flow from the vision. And leadership will always put a demand on leaders to pick the right people. . . .

Leadership also requires motivating people. And that means pushing the vision down to every level of the organization. What will make things different in the 21st century, however, is that the world is going through a transformation—a transformation that affects the industrial world as well as the political and economic world. We're moving from the Cold War era—when there was the "democratic world" and the "communist world"— to essentially "one world." At the same time, the world is being fundamentally reshaped by the information and technology revolution, which is supplanting the industrial revolution. . . . The leaders of this new industrial-information era have to be able use these tools and understand the power of information and technology—and how that gives them new opportunities. For example, our old enemies are now our competitors. They did what we told them to—they stopped building guns and facing us across borders. Instead they are competing with us in democratic systems and open markets. But even more than as competitors, we should see our old enemies as markets. Information and technology allows you to do more "niching." Industry is discovering that the power of the computer allows you to appeal to smaller and smaller markets because you are able to manufacture for smaller and smaller markets in an efficient and profitable way.

IW: Industry has entered what might be called the age of empowerment. Does this change the requisites for a company leader?

Powell: I'm always nervous about buzzwords that come along and try to capture complex ideas. But certainly any organization that is able to generate the interest of "the led" so that they contribute to the work of the organization and offer suggestions and want to be a part of what's going on—will benefit. In that sense empowerment is a good thing; companies need to do more of it. . . . We've seen [empowerment] in American industry. We've moved away from the mass [production] industrial era of Henry Ford where everyone sat on a line somewhere and did his one selected task. But I don't think empowerment is a new and revolutionary concept.

IW: Is leadership different in the military than in industry?

Powell: We [the military] are a hierarchical environment and always will be. We have the power of coercion, because we ask people to give their lives. But at the same time we are quite similar to industry. We are big on empowerment, and are big on communicating vision down to the last soldier, sailor, airman, or Marine. The fundamental principles of leadership and qualities we look for in our leaders are very parallel to what industry needs to look for.

IW: But hasn't the military changed in recent years?

Powell: We've gone for a much higher quality soldier and for much more education and training. We've sought every aspect of technology we can to make the task of the soldier easier and safer—precision weapons, for instance. We are on the cutting edge of the digital world—the information world—in order to do our terrible job of coercing people in war. Even though we are taking advantage of the new tools available, however ... we also try to teach the same kind of leadership we derive from our heroes of the past. There will always be a need for a George Washington at Valley Forge.

IW: What are the qualities of that leadership?

Powell: Beyond the qualities I talked about earlier, there are the personal qualities of courage and shared sacrifice. We teach our youngsters, for example, "If the troops are cold, you're cold. But make sure you don't look cold or act cold." Corporate leaders ought to learn that. Too often those at high levels don't quite understand the sacrifices and hardships of those at the bottom.

IW: Can leadership be learned? Or is it instinctive?

Powell: People have been talking about that for a couple thousand years. I think leadership can be shaped. You have to have some fundamental instincts for working with people. But that instinct can be improved upon through training and education, so that you understand what works for you. In my career I've come across people who were terrible leaders because they had no gut instinct for leadership and no amount of training helped them. I've also come across brilliant natural leaders who became even better when they developed their skills.

IW: Is leadership recognizable? Can it be so effective that you're not aware of it?

Powell: You recognize it in the performance of the unit. Leadership doesn't mean you have to be a "character," or wear two pistols and scream and yell a lot. Some of the most effective leaders I've seen have been quiet and unassuming, but you saw the results of their presence. The performance of the organization is the ultimate measure of a leader.

Discussion Questions

1. How would you describe General Powell's philosophy of leadership?
2. What aspects of Powell's style do you feel generalizes to all types of organizations?
3. In your opinion, which component of Powell's style differentiates him from other world-class leaders?
4. How would you relate to Powell's leadership as one of his followers? Peers? Supervisors?

3

In the Land of Cornflakes and Car Assembly*

Lee Howser, President of Jackson Community College in Jackson, Michigan, wanted to create a faculty-driven institution that was customer friendly. This required a focus both inside and outside the college. Initially more comfortable as a hands-on leader, Howser had to learn that others could take on much of the internal implementation challenges. He had to trust his intuition on how to proceed, and had to be open to new ways of operating. Howser viewed the college as part of a system. He realized early on that JCC's success would depend on the efforts of others, so he had to "stop being an implementor and work on inspiring others with the vision for change."

One Leader Takes Seriously the Need to Produce Innovative Work Systems for the Future

Lee Howser, once a television personality, is now the president of Jackson Community College (JCC) in Jackson, Michigan. While not exactly reporting the news as he once did, now he's making it at JCC. JCC is a well-known innovator among community colleges, and though he would never take the credit, Howser's leadership is undoubtedly one reason why. JCC's transformation began in the early 90s, when, as Howser puts it, "we needed to get the sand out of our gears and reach new markets." Along with others at JCC, he saw businesses facing accountability and service pressures and realized that academic settings would soon face similar challenges. Howser saw that JCC's facilities were out of date and the faculty was not prepared

---

*Katz, A. J. (1998). Quality 101. *Journal for Quality & Participation, 21*(1), 16–18. (Adapted)

for the demands that lay ahead. "We knew JCC and other academic institutions were going to be dragged through the keyhole, and we wanted Jackson to be the first one through. That was the only way we could influence the process."

Making the Move . . .

Howser, however, was not the visionary behind the original change process but considers Clyde Letarte, his predecessor, to be the leader who initiated the shift to a new direction. Howser recognized that his role was to implement the change. "It was my job to take it to the next level," he says. "I'm a mover, not a shaker. It never occurred to me not to go forward. I was interested in how."

Another person Howser credits with the vision for change is Carole Schwinn, a pioneer in the community quality movement and a staff member at JCC. Schwinn introduced some of the country's leading systems thinkers and experts in quality management to the Jackson community. But her goal was not simply education. Schwinn wanted JCC to redesign itself as a college for the future.

"She needled and nagged Clyde and me about it," Howser admits. "Her approach is a bit like Chinese water torture, and inevitably, both Clyde and I paid attention." Howser vividly remembers the moment he found the right lever for change. Along with Schwinn and others from JCC, Howser attended a workshop given by Jamshid Gharajedaghi, an expert on systems design. Gharajedaghi gave the JCC group an assignment to design a brand-new college.

"We were supposed to answer the question, 'If this were real, where are the stopping points?'" Howser recalls. "All of a sudden, we decided that we could make it real, that our 'brand-new college' could be JCC. I went back to the college and announced: 'We're going to blow this place up and start all over!'" Howser wanted to create a faculty-driven institution that was "customer-friendly." And this required a focus both inside and outside of the college. He speaks with obvious affection for the people he relied upon to help him.

"First I tried creating a 'kitchen cabinet' of close advisors who could tell me what was going on. But that just turned into a gripe session. I needed people who could be the real implementers, who could step forward and deliver the message to our faculty and staff, and who could take the heat but also see when positive things were happening."

Initially more comfortable as a hands-on leader, Howser had to learn that others could take on much of the internal implementation challenges. "They wanted me to hold the vision and to stay 'presidential,'" he explains. "They told me, 'You don't need to be doing that, but you should be doing this.' I stopped being an implementer and worked on inspiring others with the vision for change." Like many leaders, Howser had to trust his intuition on how to proceed and had to be open to new ways of operating. At times, particularly in the beginning, this became a source of conflict. "I wanted to hold a small vision session in my home, to talk with faculty and others about what our view of the future was, our common beliefs and values," he says. "I wanted to create a dialogue about where we were going. But I got talked out of it, and talked into doing a large event with lots of people. So we took two-and-a-half days; and I not only got one vision, I got three. It ended up taking six months for a team of people to edit everything so we could come up with what was really a compromise vision.

"What I got was something I didn't want: a list of projects I was supposed to take care of." Despite his disappointment, Howser's response was a defining moment in his leadership.

"One of the projects people wanted was a child-care center. I knew that the project was worthwhile because it would help us with enrollment success. But I made it clear that there were no general funds for it, and told them someone from the group would have to come forward to take it on. I told them that this was not a case of 'Daddy taking care of this.'

"Well, a group did step forward, and now we have a child care center. I provide the building only; they provide the operations. But not only that, they involved private enterprise, and that has opened some doors for us."

Mind Your Businesses . . .

As his JCC team managed the implementation process, Howser spent much of his time working with the JCC board members and stakeholders within the community. One group Howser focused on was the chamber of commerce. "I started asking [our group] questions like, 'Why don't we have a system here that serves business?' " Howser realized that there were opportunities for JCC to help create business coalitions. "I worked with the Business Alliance, and the Jackson Area Manufacturing Association brought the executive groups to the college and offered JCC as a place where they could collaborate."

The result was the formation of the Enterprise Group, a consortium of several business organizations who will eventually co-locate at JCC. Quite a few key learning experiences have shaped Howser's development. In addition to his work with Gharajedaghi, three days with Peter Senge made a real difference.

"There were two things that stood out," Howser remembers. "One was an activity called right side–left side. You write down a recent conversation in the left column. Then, on the right side, you put down what you were thinking at the time. The sides tend not to match up. That showed me, more than anything else, that I had to learn to get to the point rather than to play politics."

Senge's ideas about learning organizations also made a strong impression. "I always thought that people make things move, and that may be true. But most of us do not have a system for testing our assumptions and making adjustments.

"Four years ago, the idea of a college or organization formally taking in information, processing it, storing it, and using it was totally new to me. Now we're all making strides in learning to think in different ways."

The Bigger Picture

Howser views the college as a part of a system. He realized early on that JCC's success would depend on the health of the surrounding community and supported Carole Schwinn's dream for community partnership, thus enabling a partnership of JCC, the Jackson Area Quality Initiative (JAQI), and the W.K. Kellogg Foundation in the Jackson Community Transformation Project—which is a plan to design the ideal community. This effort on the part of JCC and the community is attracting national attention.

A great deal of work still needs to be done, particularly as the faculty develop a new curriculum and learn new ways of working together. Howser has returned to his belief in the power of communication and is now scheduling vision sessions with small groups of faculty and staff.

"This is a long, slow process, but it's important to think about the traditions we'll carry forward and the new ones we'll create."

Discussion Questions

1. To what do you attribute the changes in JCC over time, and Howser's successes at implementation?
2. Do you think he will be successful with developing the faculty and a new curriculum?
3. What behaviors or styles stand out as being related to the full range of leadership model?
4. What would you suggest to further develop Howser's style of leadership?
5. "I'm a mover, not a shaker." Explain this statement in terms of the full range of leadership model.
6. How would you relate to Howser's style of leadership as a follower? Peer? Supervisor?

4

Can You Name America's
Seven Best Bosses?*

Mary Kay Ash, Chairman Emeritus of Mary Kay Cosmetics, focuses her efforts on praising her employees. Her organization has become a Fortune 500 company, and her secret is her active attention and recognition of her employees. Jack Stack, President and CEO of Springfield Remanufacturing Corporation, focuses on empowering employees. He encourages employees to question the way things are done and how projects are financed. By asking questions and exploring the company's financial information, employees have an opportunity to increase the efficiency of the organization and hence the profit. Lawrence Bossidy is CEO of AlliedSignal. Along with his strategic business moves to sell off or consolidate several divisions, Bossidy also invested a great deal of time and money into his workforce. He implemented education and career planning strategies for his employees, and made an effort to reward those who were willing to make a commitment, show passion, and take ownership. The employees responded extraordinarily well to his efforts, as shown in subsequent organizational performance. Gun Denhart CEO of Hanna Andersson, determines what her employees want and need and provides it in order to motivate them to perform. Denhart also tries to minimize obstacles, both personal and professional; for example, Hanna Andersson pays for 50% of its employees' child-care costs. Bernard Marcus, Chairman and CEO of Home Depot, requires a lot of his employees. In return, he offers many incentives. Employees can purchase company stock 15% below market price, wages are 20% and 25% above industry average, and employees receive full health and dental benefits. The company also offers training programs to its employees, and those employees have responded to the rewarding atmosphere. Ar-

---

*Butler, C. (1994, November). The magnificent seven. *Sales & Marketing Management, Performance Supplement*, pp. 41–50. (Adapted)

thur Dunn, Director of Supply Management for Motorola Information Systems Group, has been cited for "dealing with the empowerment of people, acting as a coach and mentor, and gaining goals through strategic planning." Dunn admits that he doesn't have the answers to every problem, but he is willing to work with people to achieve a resolution. John McQiddy, President of MCQ Associates, has a management style that is inviting and stylish and a bit old-fashioned. McQiddy wants to keep his people happy by making the firm a fun place to work. He empowers employees and is flexible with them.

After talking with consultants, scanning newspapers and magazines, and surveying scores of employees, we've determined our seven supreme managers. Some names you may recognize, others you definitely won't. Some are CEOs of billion-dollar corporations, others are small-company presidents and mid-level managers. Some push their employees, some prod. Some are natural-born managers, others have honed their skills with lots of practice. For all their differences, though, they all have one thing in common: a genuine desire to enhance both the professional and personal lives of their employees. They make going to the office, to the factory "to work" an experience, not just a necessity.

Mary Kay Ash, Chairman Emeritus, Mary Kay Cosmetics, Direct Seller of Cosmetics, Dallas, Texas

Mary Kay Ash doesn't flinch at the question.

"Yes, I do think I'm a good boss because I have compassion for our people," says the founder of the cosmetics company that bears her name. "I see people, not the bottom line, as the most important thing at a company. For me, P&L stands for people and love. It's corny, but it works."

Mary Kay (she insists you call her by her first name) has a good reason why her way, corny indeed as it may sound, isn't such a bad way. This year Mary Kay Cosmetics is expected to reach revenues of more than $1 billion for the fourth consecutive year, a handsome return on the $5,000 investment Mary Kay and her late husband used to start the company in 1963. She founded the company to provide herself with secure employment and income after having been overlooked for a promotion in her previous sales position. Ultimately, she would become the first female chairman of a Fortune 500 company, with her personal worth growing to an estimated $300 million.

At age 76, Mary Kay is now chairman emeritus, with her son, Stephen, assuming full-time chairman duties. Still, she remains actively involved in the company, she can be seen almost daily in the company's Dallas headquarters talking with production workers or discussing long-term strategy with board officers. Even more apparent is her continued commitment to her 350,000 direct sellers (or individual beauty consultants), 99% of whom are women, women who, like their boss, have used Mary Kay Cosmetics to achieve a sense of professional and economic security.

Throughout the years, Mary Kay has gained the loyalty of those sellers by following a primer in management: "We praise our people to success," says Mary Kay. "And they work hard for recognition." At Mary Kay Cosmetics, recognition is as important to salespeople as a sample kit of lipstick, rouge, and mascara.

The most obvious form takes place at Seminar, the annual gathering of Mary Kay beauty consultants and directors. There, amidst glitzy giveaways and glamorous gowns, salespeople are publicly congratulated for their sales efforts over the past year. Some are given pins that read "$25,000," others that read "$100,000," and still others that read "$1 million," all designating levels of sales revenue. The pins are worn as if they were brooches from Tiffany. Then there are the Career Cars. Over the years, Mary Kay has presented to its top sellers more than 7,500 Grand Ams, Grand Prix, and pink Cadillacs worth more than $100 million.

But beyond the gifts, the women come to Seminar to hear their leader praise them with the words of a seen-it-all mother. She speaks with the comfortable voice of Dolly Parton. And yet, although her talks at Seminar can be folksy and whimsical, they are always lined with encouragement for the success these salespeople have had in a business world that can often be unfriendly to women. "What is it people say 'that the first thing a baby does when she comes into this world is cry for attention and recognition' I believe that is true," says Mary Kay. "That is how I've worked for thirty-one years—give attention and recognition where needed. I don't believe in so-called constructive criticism. I think all criticism is destructive."

In Mary Kay's world, positive reinforcement is the incentive of choice for any employees or individual. At a recent Seminar, a young boy stood near the stage, waiting for his mother to receive her words of praise from Mary Kay. When Mary Kay noticed him, she asked him what he planned to be when he grew up. He told Mary Kay and the crowd, "The first black president of the United States."

"I think the biggest legacy we are going to leave," says Mary Kay, "is a whole community of children who believe they can do anything in this world because they watched their mamas do it."

Discussion Questions

1. In what way does Mary Kay Ash display one or more of the factors of transformational and transactional leadership?
2. How much would you like to work with Mary Kay Ash?
3. How would you improve on her style of leadership?

4. What type of legacy do you believe Mary Kay Ash will leave behind?

Jack Stack, President and CEO, Springfield Remanufacturing Corp., Manufacturers of Auto Parts, Springfield, Missouri

Jack Stack asks questions, lots of them. And the employees of Springfield ReManufacturing Corp. understand why.

"Jack doesn't pretend to know all the answers to running this company, and he doesn't want to," says Gary Brown, vice president of human resources. "But when he starts asking a manager or an employee questions about how things are done or how things are going, he's really trying to help that person look for ways to make things work better. He doesn't want to give answers, he wants people to find them out for themselves."

Management by Q&A is the essence of the business mantra at Springfield ReManufacturing. Not only is the CEO always probing, he expects his employees to be, as well. Employees are encouraged to ask questions about the finances of their company—and managers are expected to provide every possible answer. The only financial information off-limits to most employees at Springfield ReManufacturing, which remanufactures car and truck engines and pumps, are the salaries and healthcare histories of fellow employees. Otherwise, all 750 employees are updated at weekly meetings with their managers on the costs and revenues, the taxes and the overhead of this $98-million company.

"What makes us significantly different from other businesses is that we financially empower our employees," says Stack, who bought Springfield ReManufacturing with 12 other managers in 1983. "Employees go through a complete education where they understand the business."

Of the more than $300,000 the company spent in training in 1993, only 14 percent went toward skills training; 86 percent was focused on training employees to be able to read company financial statements, P&L statements, debt to equity ratios. "Our dedication is to teach employees business," says Brown. "At a lot of places you hear that the customer or quality is number one. We put all emphasis in our people, because with the right training, employees will take care of the customer."

Stack credits such training for the 15 percent annual growth the company has enjoyed since the year he took over the company. And it's the cornerstone of the strategy he pitches as the Great Game of Business. In its simplest terms, the Game of Business means providing employees with the knowledge to enhance a company's production and hence its profit. Only when employees understand the rules of the game, how production affects sales, how costs and revenue determine profits, and are given a stake in the financial outcome, will a company go beyond minimal growth. Only when all employees are involved in the business will the overall success of the company become the focus of more than just the managers.

To demonstrate his point, Stack tells the story of how he visited the company's maintenance department a few years ago. He asked Don Wood, a supervisor, how the financial training was working. Wood didn't hesitate. "We used to be one of the most political departments in the company," he told Stack. "We had power, because we decided who got help first when something needed fixing and it was usually the people we liked that we took care of. But since we got the financials, we look at who's having trouble and fix them first. Because if they're working right, we're all making money." For Stack, the game of business is not just providing more money for employees. It's providing more understanding. "Millions and millions of people are going to work each day not knowing how business works," says Stack, who often spends weekends fishing with his employees. "They know how to do their jobs, but have no methods where they can significantly control the outcome and the profits of the company. Management assumes employees can do only simple tasks.

"People unify under a financial statement," he says. "It knocks down the walls."

Discussion Questions

1. In what way does Jack Stack display one or more of the factors of transformational and transactional leadership?
2. How much would you like to work with Jack Stack?
3. How would you improve on his style of leadership?

Lawrence A. Bossidy, CEO, AlliedSighal, Aerospace and Automotive Parts Manufacturer, Morristown, New Jersey

Working in the shadow of the boss of bosses, General Electric's Jack Welch, for 10 years, Larry Bossidy probably had to wonder some nights driving home from work if he would ever get the chance to run a company, and how he would do it if he got the chance.

In 1991, Bossidy, at the age of 56, finally earned the opportunity. And since becoming CEO of AlliedSignal that year, he has proven that he has the credentials to be not only a chief executive, but also a great one. Before the eyes of Wall Street, executive recruiters, and most importantly his employees, he has helped reinvigorate the aerospace and automotive parts manufacturer. AlliedSignal's stock value has more than doubled since his arrival, and its 1993 net income of $411 million was a marked reversal from the company's $273 million loss in 1991. Such improvements did not come without tough decisions, and Bossidy, known to work with swiftness, made a number of moves that seemed right out of Jack Welch's management handbook. He either sold off or consolidated several AlliedSignal divisions, and reduced the company's workforce by 14,000.

But while the moves were necessary for AlliedSignal's financial future, Bossidy also invested money, and his own time, in the 85,000 remaining employees. He introduced programs intended to be intellectually stimulating to employees, and that would prepare many of them to become the next generation of AlliedSignal managers and executives. As he told *Business Week* shortly after taking the job, "I want to identify people who have passion, who are willing to make a commitment, take ownership, and make it a premier company."

Toward that end, Bossidy immediately called for all employees to go through a total quality management program. Employees attended a four-day course during which they looked at and began to solve real-case problems in their work areas. He also backed a program in which employees were asked to fill out forms listing such items as their career goals and what other divisions they would consider working in. A database was compiled from the information in order to identify employees with career aspirations that could be filled when an opening became available in the company.

For Bossidy, the education and career planning strategies were similar to ones his parents forced him to follow as an 18-year-old. At the time, he received a $40,000-a-year offer to pitch for the Detroit Tigers. His parents, who owned a Massachusetts shoe store, convinced him that a scholarship offer from Colgate University was a better investment long term.

Beyond investing in his employees, Bossidy has also played a part in lifting the spirits of a lethargic, almost stagnant company. He ordered a corporate vision statement to be written, did away with preferred parking areas, and made Fridays in the summer half days. He also holds frequent meetings with employee groups, and is often seen waiting in line in the employee cafeteria.

Small gestures? Sure, but also effective ones. "When I came here, a lot of people were very dispirited," Bossidy told *Financial World* earlier this year. "People had no idea where they were going." And now they don't have to worry about their boss going anywhere. Because of the swiftness and magnitude of AlliedSignal's turnaround, Bossidy has been courted by executive recruiters of several companies, most notably IBM. Last August, in a move to keep predators at bay, AlliedSignal signed Bossidy to a new contract that will pay the CEO a base salary of $2 million annually.

Discussion Questions

1. In what way does Lawrence A. Bossidy display one or more of the factors of transformational and transactional leadership?

2. How much would you like to work with Lawrence A. Bossidy?

3. How would you improve on his style of leadership?

4. Is someone like Lawrence A. Bossidy "born to lead," or made? Why?

Gun Denhart, CEO, Hanna Andersson, Maker
of Mail-Order Children's Clothes, Portland, Oregon

You think the world of direct mail is as easy as licking an envelope? Think again.

One Saturday morning eight years ago, when Helena Grotte arrived at the suburban Portland home of her boss, Gun Denhart, the breakfast dishes hadn't even been cleared from the kitchen table. But during the next 48 hours, the two natives of Sweden, along with "as many kids as we could find in the neighborhood," as Grotte recalls, took turns gluing patches of sample cloth into 25,000 mail-order catalogues. The catalogues, which featured the Hanna Andersson children's clothes line Denhart had originated two years earlier, needed to be in the mail by Monday morning.

"I don't know how we did it," recalls Grotte in her soft Swedish accent, "but we sat and glued and glued until we got it done."

From those patchwork beginnings, when she had just a dozen or so employees working for her in her home, Denhart has weaved Hanna Andersson into one of the country's most successful mail-order ventures. The company now employs 260 people and occupies a five-story building in downtown Portland. It also operates a distribution center in Kentucky. Last year, the company had revenues of $40 million. Its line of mostly children's clothing is noted for being made of 100 percent cotton, and fashioned after the style of Denhart's homeland.

Throughout the growth, though, Denhart (who founded the company with her husband, Tom) has remained loyal to running her company with the philosophy that work should be just one patch in the fabric of an employee's life.

The company's employee benefit package has produced a mutual desire between employer and employee to give back. For instance, despite its relatively small size, Hanna Andersson pays for 50 percent of its employees' child-care costs. Last year, the perk cost the company $250,000. "I think at the time we started the child-care benefit, it was a radical idea," Denhart, 48, and a mother of three children, says. "But I knew some of the people who worked for us weren't making that much money and they had children. It was something we needed to do."

Another distinguishing company promotion is the Hannadown Program. Customers who return their used children's garments receive a 20-percent credit. Hanna Andersson, in turn, donates the clothing to local charities. It also donates 5 percent of its annual pre-tax profits to company-chosen charities.

What are Denhart's motives behind such acts of charity? Motivation. That may seem to be convoluted logic, but since the late 1960s when she studied for her business degree in Sweden, the subject of what pushes people to work has intrigued Denhart. "While everyone else was writing their theses on cost analysis and such, I was writing mine on what motivated people," says Denhart. The answer she found is the principle she still adheres to. "I approach life with the outlook that people want to do a good job."

According to Denhart, employees can't accomplish this goal unless obstacles "both personal and professional" are minimized. Such thinking prompted the company's childcare benefit and contributed to a corporate culture similar to the kinship found in a large family.

"Gun is very honest and direct, which isn't the case with many American executives," say Grotte, now a Hanna Andersson buyer. "She gives you encouragement." But like most families, Hanna Andersson has had its troubles, and it was Denhart who was searching for encouragement in 1993 when the company experienced its first nondouble-digit-growth year. Denhart and company officials were forced to make moves that severely affected the welfare and morale of employees. Twenty employees were laid off, and such benefits as free parking and 100 percent employee health coverage were discontinued.

"It was pretty scary for a while," says Denhart. "It has changed the culture here a bit, and we look at how we do things differently."

The company has since financially righted itself, and 19 of the 20 dismissed employees have been rehired. While employees must now pay $50 a month for parking and for 8 percent of their health coverage, the child-care benefit remains intact. And Denhart dismisses talk that the company had these problems because "we were unconscientious." Ultimately, she says, it's the inspiration an employer provides, not necessarily the financial benefits, that allows employees to accomplish the goal of doing a good job. At Hanna Andersson, each new employee receives a 10-point "How to be Happy at Hanna" tipsheet that features such hints as "never stop growing," "stay away from office politics," and "bring energy to work." Denhart's favorite is tip number six: keep a balance between work and play. Says Denhart, "I have kids that I like to see."

Discussion Questions

1. In what way does Gun Denhart display one or more of the factors of transformational and transactional leadership?
2. How much would you like to work with Gun Denhart?
3. How would you improve on her style of leadership?

4. How would Gun Denhart's entrepreneurial leadership style work in a
   very established, conservative organization?

Bernard Marcus, Chairman and CEO, Home Depot,
National Chain of Home-Repair Supply Stores,
Atlanta, Georgia

Ernie Palisin talks about Home Depot faster than a race track announcer
calls a horse race. That's because Palisin loves his job, and the company he
works for. "Home Depot treats its customers and its employees right,"
Palisin, supervisor of plumbing at an Orlando, Florida, Home Depot, gushes.
"And that's because Bernie's enthusiasm makes a difference. He works with
you, not against."

Bernard Marcus, who founded the supply store chain in 1978 and has
watched it blossom to more than 300 stores nationwide and in Canada ($9.2
billion in sales), is credited with making shopping for lawn mowers, carpet-
ing, fertilizer, and other household goods enjoyable as well as easy, even
though the stores themselves can be as monstrous as airplane hangars.

Why? Because Marcus founded the business with a mandate that employees treat customers like fine pieces of china, and then gave those employees the training, the financial incentives, and the encouragement to fulfill his demand. "Bernie Marcus has a view on how to treat employees that
puts him in a different class," says J. Anthony Clancy, a partner at Andersen
Consulting in Atlanta. "He has high expectations of his people, but also involves them."

One way Marcus has insured such all-around treatment is by not paying
salespeople on commission. Instead, employees can purchase Home Depot
stock at 15 percent below market price, a plan that has paid significant dividends in recent years. Home Depot wages are reportedly 20 percent to 25
percent above industry averages. In addition, employees receive full health
and dental benefits.

The company offers more than 30 formalized training programs, some of
which seem almost sacrilegious but have still garnered the devotion employees. Two Sundays each month, employees arrive at their stores two
hours before opening for Product Knowledge classes. During these classes
vendors instruct employees on how to sell and service their products. Also
on periodic Sundays, Marcus and Home Depot President and COO Arthur
Blank are seen coast to coast via a closed-circuit television program called
"Breakfast with Bernie and Art." During the program, the two chief officers
speak to their employees from one of their stores, updating them on corporate news and answering their questions.

Need proof that employees and customers respond to this atmosphere
Marcus has created? A while back, Palisin designed an irrigation system for

Don Bianco, a customer living on the outskirts of Orlando. Shortly after installing the system, though, Bianco was transferred by his company to Tennessee. When he arrived at his new home and wanted to install an irrigation system there, whom did he call? Palisin. "He sent me designs of his house and I faxed him back designs of an irrigation system," Palisin says matter-of-factly. "At Home Depot, we think of ourselves as a school for our customers and I'm the teacher."

The teachers have been taught very well.

Discussion Questions

1. In what way does Bernard Marcus display one or more of the factors of transformational and transactional leadership?
2. How much would you like to work with Bernard Marcus?
3. How would you improve on his style of leadership?
4. How does Bernard Marcus create a learning organization, and what other techniques would you recommend?

Arthur Dunn, Director of Supply Management, Motorola Information Systems Group, Mansfield, Massachusetts

Arthur Dunn was supposed to get two minutes of overtime to go with his official 15 minutes of fame. Then Nolan Ryan got in the way.

Last July 28, Dunn, the director of supply management for a unit of Motorola Inc., received word that he had been named America's Best Boss in the second annual Best Boss/Worst Boss Contest. More than 325 employees nominated their bosses for the Best Boss portion of the contest, conducted by Jim Miller, the CEO of a Dallas-based furniture supply company and author of *The Corporate Coach*. In selecting Dunn, Miller cited him for "dealing with empowerment of people, acting as a coach and mentor, and gaining goals through strategic planning."

Minutes after Dunn found out, and for weeks thereafter, he was swamped with interview requests and congratulatory wishes. The Associated Press. *The Providence Journal*. Several Boston TV stations. Even the CEO of Motorola stopped by Dunn's office to see him.

But the highlight came when NBC invited Dunn and Miller to make a Labor Day appearance on "The Today Show." Dunn, who had reluctantly accepted much of the attention, nonetheless was looking forward to a morning with Bryant and Katie, that is, until NBC canceled their appearance in favor of Ryan, the former baseball star. Was Dunn disappointed? Sure, but if someone had to replace him, he could appreciate it being an athlete.

Dunn, a Motorola manager for 12 years, has adhered to the principles he learned as a high school basketball and football player growing up in Easton, Massachusetts. "I don't look upon myself as bossing people around. I look at myself as coaching people," says Dunn, who oversees a staff of 50 people involved in purchasing and computer engineering for the company's data communication equipment. "I'm coaching a group of individuals and making sure we have the proper vision and are allocating our resources to support the initiative of the corporation."

That style has made an impression on Jim Limperis, the employee who nominated Dunn for the Best Boss title. In his entry letter, Limperis made a list of his boss's chief qualities creating the acronym LEADER: Dunn is a Listener and is Equitable; he Anticipates and Delegates; he is an Exceptional strategist as well as a Realist. "I think Jim pinned me down pretty well," says Dunn. "I don't have all the answers to problems. I really provide insight into what the potential problems might be and work with people to get the resolution."

Discussion Questions

1. In what way does Arthur Dunn display one or more of the factors of transformational and transactional leadership?
2. How much would you like to work with Arthur Dunn?
3. How would you improve on his style of leadership?
4. How does leadership experiences in sports contribute to leadership development in business?

John McQiddy, President, MCQ Associates, Research and Development Company, Fredericksburg, Virginia

MCQ Associates has style. Walk through the company's offices in Fredericksburg, Virginia, 30 minutes south of Washington D.C., and the first thing you'll notice are the desks. Hand-crafted, oak-made desks. All antiques. And every employee, from receptionist to president, has one.

"It makes the place a lot more comfortable-looking than a bunch of cubicles," says John McQuiddy, president of MCQ Associates, where even the filing cabinets are made of oak, not steel. "I think it's a lot more fun to work in this kind of atmosphere." Such a setting, relaxed, comfortable, but still functional, is what McQuiddy has tried to develop at his 10-year-old company, which provides security and surveillance research for the U.S. Defense Department and such commercial customers as Westinghouse and TRW.

But it's not the furniture that most of MCQ's 17 employees will first speak of when discussing McQuiddy, or the cruise-ship parties up the Potomac

River to which employees and their families are invited after MCQ closes a big deal, or the free soda in the company cafeteria. What they initially mention is a management style that is inviting and stylish and a bit old-fashioned. Sort of like the desks.

"His philosophy is, you get good people and keep them happy by making it a fun place to work," says Debra Flanigen, who started with the company seven years ago as a secretary and is now its accountant.

How does McQuiddy do it? In practical terms, he will pay the full cost of any educational course an employee takes that will benefit his or her career. In emotional terms, he allows for flexible work hours. Earlier this year, after Flanigen gave birth to her third child, McQuiddy approved a plan that lets her work in the office only three days a week. Last year, when the child of an MCQ programmer became severely ill, McQuiddy gave the employee as much time off as he needed, with full pay. And in business terms, he discusses MCQ's financial situation with employees at regularly scheduled meetings.

Why such flexibility and openness on his part? "People can't do their work unless they can concentrate on their work," McQuiddy says. "You can be draconian as a manager, but you will never create the team atmosphere that you need. You build a team by stressing positives, not negatives, and looking out for everyone's interests. But most important, you let your employees know what your vision is so everyone can work to get there."

That team approach came into play last summer. MCQ, which has spent much of the past two years in transition from a company that relies on defense department contracts to one that caters to commercial suppliers, faced a financial crunch. One June afternoon, McQuiddy gathered his employees. "We're going to lose money this month," he told them, and then gave them two options: Everyone, including himself, would need to take a 10 percent pay cut, or he would have to initiate layoffs. Their response: We'll take the pay cut.

The upside to the story: In July, when business picked up, McQuiddy reinstated the salaries.

No one had to clear out his or her desk.

Discussion Questions

1. In what way does John McQuiddy display one or more of the factors of transformational and transactional leadership?
2. How much would you like to work with John McQuiddy?
3. How would you improve on his style of leadership?
4. How does John McQuiddy's style fit with the needs of the current generation of employees coming into the workforce?

5

Leading by Listening

During Barbara Roberts' term as governor of Oregon, she had "Conversation with Oregon," interactive televised discussions between the governor and thousands of Oregonians. The dialogue sessions included the governor's illustrated presentation on state revenues and expenditures and the impact of Measure 5, a citizens' initiative restricting local property tax rates. Roberts attempted to work with people and tried to get them involved in decision making. She suggests that her collaborative leadership style stems at least in part from her desire to listen and collaborate with the people in the community.

PART I. BARBARA ROBERTS' CONVERSATION WITH OREGON*

Executives describe pragmatic reasons for their move toward collaborative management. Many note their frustration with "lack of buy-in" from their staffs during organizational decision making. Collaboration simply appears to be more effective. Says David Leclaire, "I've become much more collaborative. I graduated from the Air Force Academy and was trained in command and control management. Now, I try hard to work with people and get them involved in decision making. I want people to feel an ownership of decisions. If they don't buy in, they won't support the decision. The days of command and control are over." Other government executives agree.

---

*Johnson, G., & Johnson, N. (1996). Leading by listening: Barbara Roberts; conversation with Oregon. *Government Executive, 28*(9), 42–43. (Adapted)

The Best Leaders Know How to Listen. But Few Elected Officials Have Had as Much Experience as Oregon's Former Governor at Using Conversation as a Tool for Change

The same day Oregonians elected Democrat Barbara Roberts governor, they passed a citizens initiative restricting local property tax rates. Ballot Measure 5 also required the state to replace all revenue lost by schools and local governments because of the new rate cap. The result? A projected $2.6 billion cost to state government over five years. "It was the shortest honeymoon in history," Roberts says of her election night. "I didn't even get a kiss."

But Roberts was undaunted, determined to manage the first round of cuts from the state's $7 billion general fund budget and tackle tax reform. The governor chose collaboration as her core strategy to reengage citizens and build consensus on the tough choices the state faced in 1991. And the key to collaboration was communication. A "Conversation" is how Barbara Roberts scored some first-year wins, including legislative concurrence on key elements of her first-year agenda and an initial round of Measure 5-driven budget cuts. She worked with communities, businesses—and her former opponent for governor—to refine and win legislative endorsement of the bottom-up "Oregon Benchmarks" strategic planning and management process, begun by her Democratic predecessor.

When a second payment was due on the voter-driven tax caps, editorial and political pressures built for Roberts to adopt a "quick-fix solution" to the growing gap between revenues and spending: a tax reform ballot measure that she believed would fail. Says Roberts, "I could have called it the 'Roberts Reform Package.' It would have sounded like leadership, smelled like leadership, looked like leadership. Editorials across my state would have heralded my actions. And when it was rejected by the voters, they would have said, 'nice try.' But we wouldn't have been one step closer to a solution."

Roberts knew that undertaking such a complex issue—one that must eventually be resolved at the ballot box—required early and broadly representative participation by Oregonians.

Thus was born Roberts' "Conversation with Oregon," a high-tech grassroots dialogue between the governor and thousands of Oregonians about the future of the state.

Randomly selected registered voters were invited to participate in interactive televised discussions with the governor. Roberts personally led 32 two-hour sessions broadcast through the state's telecommunications network, Ed-Net. Each broadcast connected the governor to about 30 sites around the state. More than 10,000 citizens eventually traveled to local studios to "meet" the governor on live video and engage in a dialogue through an audio system that enabled speakers to be heard by participants at the other sites.

"Sometimes the rooms are packed. Sometimes only the moderator shows up," reported Portland's *Willamette Week* in December 1991. "But no matter how small her audience, Roberts never fails to turn on the charisma. Picture a combination of Judy Garland, Thomas Jefferson and Billy Graham."

The sessions included the governor's illustrated presentation on state revenues and expenditures—and the impact of Measure 5. Citizens exchanged views on how well state government was spending their money, the level of state services they wanted, and how the state should pay for those services. Groups then shared their opinions with the governor and other participants.

The Conversation only revved up the critics' rhetoric: "Some states have a governor," wrote an editor at Oregon's largest daily newspaper. "Oregon has a weather person." But most participants found the Conversation worthwhile. A University of Oregon survey found that participants not only learned more about state finances, but felt the Conversation "offered hope for citizen influence in the policy-making process." Roberts held another round of face-to-face meetings with voters, then carefully crafted what she termed a "balanced" tax reform package. The governor hoped that her "citizen-designed" tax package—with a boost from her state restructuring and downsizing initiatives—would meet with voter approval. She called a special legislative session to place the measure on the ballot.

The tax package passed the Democrat-controlled Senate, but lost in the Republican-controlled House by two votes. It never reached the voters. "We did a great job of bringing everybody to the table, we did a great job of designing a reform program," Roberts said in an interview at the end of her term. "We did a wonderful job of bringing people aboard—business, churches, and community leaders. But I failed to do as effective a job as I could have with the legislature." Seal, chief management officer at the Pension Benefit Guaranty Corporation, recalls that he used to deal with agency offices separately. "Now, I try to bring people together from all across the agency to get different viewpoints," he says. "We no longer live in a stovepipe world. I've seen too much 'we versus them' mentality in government. We need to shift to 'we and we.' "

Discussion Questions

1. What else could Barbara Roberts have done to add to the effectiveness of her "Conversations"?
2. How would you characterize Barbara Roberts' FRL style?
3. How would you like to work with Barbara Roberts? Why?

PART II. COLLABORATING

David Leclaire, who is responsible for program support in the Department of Energy's Office of Defense Programs, uses the budget process as an illustration of the need for increased participation in decision making: "We have a budget of $3.5 billion, but it is going to get smaller. There is going to be increased competition for scarce resources and there are a lot of people who want part of that budget. We are going to have to examine different approaches to getting our job done and we are going to need new ways to work out our differences."

Although the term *empowerment* has become part of management lingo, executives described their new relationship with employees in terms of collaboration and partnership. The new leadership appears to be moving away from hierarchy and toward peer relationships. Employees are seen as partners and collaborators, not underlings to be empowered.

The role of collaborator also signifies a significant departure for many who grew up and prospered in the traditional bureaucracy in which they alone were responsible for their work. Many described the difficulty of delegating. They found the transition from hands-on leadership to hands-off emotionally traumatic. Many began collaborating as a way to stay involved in work and add value—while still letting go. "As I moved up in the organization, I realized I couldn't make all the decisions myself," says Jill Lytle, a deputy assistant secretary at the Energy Department. "It was a real struggle to find the right balance as to when to delegate and what bounds to set. Over time, I learned to identify more and more situations where I could delegate and became more comfortable with my new role." The new leadership is also characterized by a genuine desire by executives to develop the people who report to them. They say they want to be mentors and coaches, not bosses. Listen to Lynn Wigbels, assistant director for international programs at NASA: "My job is to help people grow. I have to challenge people to do things that they haven't done in the past."

Michael J. Cocchiola, director of the Defense Printing Service, calls coaching, cheerleading, and mentoring his most important jobs. "I am trying to create leaders within our organization. I want to get the right people and bring them along as leaders." The executives all talked about the importance of understanding people's individual concerns. "I've learned you to have to pay attention to people on an individual basis," says Lytle. "You need to understand their needs and connect with them. This is especially important in a technical agency like Energy, when you may forget about the people part of your job."

Another government executive views coaching as a cornerstone of the new leadership. He said it's not enough to focus on people's individual development needs. "The job of the leader is to increasingly create the right environment which brings out the best in people and allows them to do their best work," he notes. True leaders do more than nurture their organizations and staffs. They make things happen. They act "as the stimulus in bringing about or hastening a result," as one dictionary defines the catalyst's role. Other executives speak passionately about the need to set the organization's vision and serve as the driving force for achieving it. Daniel Beard, former commissioner of the Bureau of Reclamation, describes his evolution: "I couldn't manage an organization of 8,000 people. I had to be a leader. I had to provide inspiration and a sense of direction. I had to set the tone." During his tenure at Reclamation, Beard led a major reinvention effort, which included downsizing by 1,500 employees, eliminating management layers, closing offices, and radically restructuring the agency's goals and business processes. Cocchiola emphasizes the need for persistence and consistency in advocating the vision. "You can't deviate from the vision," he states. "Your challenge is to get everybody marching toward the vision."

As with the collaborator role, the catalyst role also involves letting go of work you have done previously. "I realized that my new job is to provide leadership and direction rather than doing the job itself," says James Milhoan, a deputy executive director at the Nuclear Regulatory Commission.

A major part of the catalyst role is thinking strategically. "My role," explains Tom Dausch, director of the Office of Personnel Management's Eastern Management Development Center, "is to think strategically about where my operation has to be down the road. While part of my job is to acknowledge and accept the fine work that is being done now, the major part of my job is to think three to five years ahead." Dausch's challenge is to keep the center's curriculum relevant to the learning needs of federal executives so the center can stay competitive.

Catalysts are activists, because creating an organizational vision is a collaborative rather than a solitary endeavor. Executives describe it as an ongoing, active process in which they serve as chief nag to drive and inspire their organization toward a lofty goal or new future. The catalyst can't get the job done alone, notes Malcolm Peterson, NASA comptroller. "You need people who worry about the trains running on time. You need to combine the power of people who are visionaries with people who make things happen every day. Visionaries need people who have the ability to focus on nuts and bolts."

A broad range of collaborative abilities are needed by executives in today's government. Federal officials interviewed by *Government Executive* observed that modern leaders must be flexible and adaptable, willing to take risks, and articulate with enthusiasm the enduring values and current missions of the organizations they serve.

Looking ahead toward a new generation of government leaders, a long-term effort is needed to develop a more broadly educated cadre of high-level officials that are more similar to the British senior service than to any American counterpart. Government will need far more carefully crafted arrangements and leadership for change and renewal. Collaborating executives will need (1) initiative and the willingness to exercise discretionary authority; (2) a preference for autonomy as a work style; (3) strong intellectual abilities, shaped by a broad liberal education as well as strong technical skills; and (4) a strong motivation to serve the public.

Discussion Questions

1. What full range of leadership styles are illustrated by David Leclaire, Jill Lytle, Lynn Wigbels, Michael Cocchiola, Daniel Beard, James Milhoan, Malcolm Peterson, and Tom Dausch?
2. Which of these leaders would you enjoy working for most? Why?

6

Patricia Gallup, CEO,
PC Connection (Excerpts)*

Gallup is known not only for her determination but also her ability to nurture her employees and provide consistent, top-notch customer service. The success of PC Connection can be explained largely by its ability to produce continuous innovations and its commitment to putting the customers first. When employees are encouraged to enter into partnerships and learn with others inside and outside the organization, innovative ideas multiply. PC Connection has such partnerships with customers, suppliers, and the community; Gallup has motivated employees help to fulfil those partnerships.

David Hall, the former CEO of the computer mail-order firm PC Connection, vividly recalls the event that convinced him Patricia Gallup would be a great business partner. Back in 1979, for an anthropology course during her senior year at the University of Connecticut, Gallup had to create an authentic tepee from scratch. This involved debarking over a dozen tree trunks, something that took Gallup an entire week. "She chose to remove all that bark manually, using an old-fashioned drawshave," recalls Hall, who first met Gallup on a hiking trip when she was 21 and he was 26. "By the end of it, her fingers were bloody and blistered."

Patricia Gallup, now the 44-year-old chief executive of the $500-million-a-year business she and Hall founded in 1982, is clearly tenacious. But this is only one of the qualities that makes her a great leader. When *Working*

---

*Wachs, E. (1998). Leadership for the millennium. *Working Woman*, 23(3), pp. 28–34. (Adapted)

Woman set out several months ago to explore the issue of business leadership for the 21st century, we spoke to over a dozen experts, including management consultants, executives, and authors. We asked who they thought best exemplified first-class leadership in corporate America. Many of them pointed to Gallup, citing not only her determination but also her ability to nurture her employees and provide consistent, top-notch customer service.

In fact, they say, Gallup represents a whole new breed of corporate leader. CEOs can no longer tap their company's full potential using a command/control style. With words like integration, consensus, collaboration, and teamwork being tossed around, the model for great leadership is undergoing a sea change. The next generation of leaders will be those who can build a vision based on awareness of economic change, then help their partners and staff fulfill that vision. Patricia Gallup has done just that. As Patricia Aburdene, co-author of *Megatrends for Women*, puts it, "Gallup is not a throwback to the industrial era. Leaders who spark people today don't just tell others what to do. The struggle is more about how to invest in a well-educated work force, then develop effective ways to mine their brain power. The key to this is catalyzing your resources."

Since Gallup is a new-style leader, her success hasn't come in a conventional way. For one thing, she doesn't fit the profile of a typical high-tech entrepreneur. Her headquarters isn't in Silicon Valley but in the unlikely locale of Milford, New Hampshire, where horses and deer graze nearby. She didn't go to Stanford University, the alma mater of many tech moguls, and, of course, she doesn't have an engineering degree. In fact, she credits her background in anthropology with helping her put her business on the map. "My knowledge of primitive cultures taught me a lot about how people use tools and what effect they have on their development," says Gallup. "Although the tools may be different today, the principles are similar. In the computer industry, you always need to think about what technology the customer will need in the future."

In 1982, Gallup was thinking about how personal computers, which had just hit the market, would shape consumers' lives. Twenty-eight years old and working with David Hall as a project manager in his family's electronics business, Gallup was fascinated by the PC revolution and decided to invest some of her savings in a personal computer. That's when she discovered that the nearest computer merchant was almost three hours away. If she could have this problem in southern New Hampshire, she wondered how far other consumers might have to go to get a machine. Then there was the matter of the computer sales staff in electronics stores. Most were techies who spoke a language the average consumer didn't understand.

Though she had no experience in high tech, Gallup saw a business opportunity. **Why not sell computers and peripherals through mail order?** At a time when retail stores had only just begun to stock PCs, this was a radical notion. Would people really buy one of these expensive gadgets sight unseen? Gallup thought so, especially if she could offer consumers better sales support and more information than they were getting in retail stores.

Gallup approached Hall, who had an electrical engineering background. She convinced him that she could rustle up business if he could handle the technical side of things—like picking which computers the company would sell and training a sales staff to troubleshoot on the phone. Hall agreed, and the pair set to work. Within a year, they were busy enough to quit their day jobs.

"I learned a long time ago not to listen when someone says I can't," explains Gallup, a tall, thin blonde with serene blue eyes, now perched behind the long, wooden desk in her corner office at company headquarters. "I knew from the start I'd be successful."

Gallup and Hall put up $8,000 and advertised PC Connection in computer and general business magazines. With a handful of staff on phone support and a wholesale stock of several thousand dollars' worth of products for IBM PCs that Gallup had uncovered by poring over computer magazines, a company was born. In 1987, *Inc.* magazine declared PC Connection to be the second-fastest growing company in the U.S. In 1990, after the business had taken off, Hall scaled back his daily responsibilities and now contributes to PC Connection primarily as a board member. Gallup moved from the presidency into the CEO's job, taking over many of the tasks that were formerly her partner's.

"One of the biggest trends in leadership today is direct communication, because it mirrors the very technology we use to work. The Web is an apt title. Leaders in the next century will lead from the center, gleaning the best ideas from those around them, not from the top."

THE FEMALE ADVANTAGE: WOMEN'S WAYS OF LEADERSHIP

When it comes to leadership, Patricia Gallup has always been ahead of the curve. For starters, PC Connection is devoid of the bureaucracy that typically comes with growth. Gallup's open and accessible style has a lot to do with that. Even with 824 employees on board, she communicates directly with most of them, either in person or via e-mail, which she starts sending at 5:30 in the morning. As she walks through the hallways of the office, she greets most employees by name.

The ease of communication within PC Connection is one of the company's major advantages. The customer service and sales departments meet each week with product managers to discuss specific problems customers may have had with computers and software. The sales staff also checks in with corporate clients on a daily basis, then updates service and product managers. This information flows to Gallup, who then holds weekly meetings with human resources, corporate communications, legal, and operations. After those meetings, Gallup and Hall discuss tech trends, ways to enhance internal efficiency, and business strategies. Every week, Gallup e-mails all department heads, outlining the company's progress. Anyone who wants to address a problem can simply walk over to her office, which is in a central pod rather than an executive suite. Gallup's door is always open, and Oriental rugs and leather chairs are noticeably absent. Instead, there is a nondescript dark green carpet and a wooden desk, where she keeps her Macintosh Duo Dock and IBM ThinkPad notebook. A space heater rumbles in the corner of the room, and the only decoration is a vase of fake flowers. "I just haven't had much time to fix up my office," she says with a laugh.

No wonder all that communication and accessibility take up most of her day. One thing that hasn't changed about corporate leadership is that it's hard work. Gallup is trying to scale down to a 60-hour week, so she can spend time with her husband, Randall Minard, an optometrist; the two enjoy hiking, cross-country skiing, and Irish folk dancing in their limited free time. Many people believe that scaling back will be good not only for Gallup, but for PC Connection as well. Jennifer Starr, a visiting research scholar at Wellesley and the author of *Women Entrepreneurs: A Review of Current Research*, notes that Gallup runs PC Connection like a family business. "She's a micro-manager. She could have grown the company faster, but up until now she wanted to stay private and keep her 50 percent ownership."

That safe strategy may have protected the company from outsiders in its infancy, but it also allowed competitors like Michael Krasny, who runs CDW, a rival computer reseller, to move into PC Connection's territory. "Ten years ago, we were the little guy next to PC Connection," says Krasny. "But since then, we've grown faster than them and our repeat business is higher than theirs—over 70 percent."

Gallup would argue that the advantage of having tight control over her business is that she can move PC Connection in a radical direction at a moment's notice, and be reasonably sure her employees will follow. In the mercurial world of high tech, this is a big plus. For example, in 1992, Gallup decided to move PC Connection's distribution center from a New Hampshire mill town to the cornfields of Wilmington, Ohio. Gallup's tech department had come up with a way to configure custom-made products overnight, and she wanted to be able to take advantage of the new technology with overnight shipping. The company's shipper, Airborne Express, was located in Wilmington, but many of PC Connection's distribution managers had never left New Hampshire. Still, all 12 were willing to relocate to Ohio. "I moved myself, my wife, four kids, one cow, three horses, and six dogs and cats," says Don Kincaid, the head of distribution. "It was like Noah's ark driving across the New York State Thruway." Kincaid says he was willing to move because Gallup told him about the plan immediately and involved him in making decisions about the transition. There were no surprises. He adds, "I wouldn't have done it if I wasn't excited about how vibrant and alive the company was, and still is."

That employees are willing to jump through such hoops is good news for Gallup, as she plans to move company headquarters this summer for the third time in as many years to Merrimack, New Hampshire, less than 10 miles away from the current headquarters. Gallup hopes the move will allow her to tap into talent from nearby Nashua, where there is a large concentration of workers with technical skills. In addition, the city was recently ranked by *Money* magazine as the best city in the United States to live in and do business.

How do you keep good people while keeping an eye on the bottom line? That's the major business challenge today. Leaders have to recognize that the perks have changed. In the 1980s, you gave people hefty expense accounts to wine and dine clients. Now, you give them a learning budget for specialized training. And the flexibility to get the job done. Punching the clock is passe. Business leaders have to learn that a staff is paid to think, not just to do."

GOING PUBLIC*

The IPO will also offer Gallup another competitive edge: stock options. Most skilled employees at high tech companies expect options as part of their compensation package, and Gallup says that providing equity to attract and retain good people was her main reason for going public. She wants to turn workers into shareholders, and perhaps even create some options millionaires, as companies like Microsoft and Netscape have done. "It's the perfect link between performance of employees and rewards," says Matt Ward, whose San Francisco consulting firm, WestWard Pay Strategies, designs stock plans for technology companies. "And it's become the currency of choice in the field." Those options, and the extra cash generated by the IPO, may be just the thing that PC Connection needs to raise its profile and take its place beside those well-known, fast-growing Silicon Valley tech firms.

Discussion Questions

1. Many pioneers fail in what becomes a competitive industry. To what full range of leadership factors do you attribute Patricia Gallup's success?

---

*Wachs, E. (1998). Going public. *Working Woman, 23*(3), 34.

2. What do you think will happen to PC Connection when Patricia Gallup scales back personally?
3. How would you describe the type of culture that has been created at PC Connection, based on what you know about Gallup's style of leadership?

7

Global Leadership*

In an interview, Robert J. Eaton, chairman and CEO of Chrysler Corporation, dis-
cussed management styles and the automobile industry. According to Eaton, he
and former Chrysler chairman Lee Iacocca are very different people. Whereas
Iacocca leaned toward sales and marketing and was known worldwide, Eaton is
an engineer who tries to build teams and prefers not to stand out. Eaton believes
that through building teams and empowering people, the automaker can accom-
plish its goals. The culture of Chrysler is very similar to that of General Motors
(GM) Europe, where Eaton served as president from June 1988 until he left the
company in March 1992. In a global market, companies will be more competi-
tive if they work together with the government, as opposed to working as adver-
saries. According to Eaton, Chrysler is making good progress in getting more
women and minorities into key line positions. Eaton does not want managers; he
looks for leaders.

Legendary Chrysler Chairman Lee A. Iacocca announced his impending retirement in late 1991, triggering a global search for his successor. Chrysler's
board of directors selected Robert J. Eaton, 53, a long-time General Motors
executive and, like Iacocca, an engineer by training.

Eaton, the son of a brakeman and a beauty operator, joined GM in 1963
as a college graduate-in-training at Chevrolet Motor Division's Engineering
Center in Warren, MI. He spent nearly three decades with the automaker in
a variety of engineering and management assignments, ultimately serving

---

*Lienert, A. (1994). The man in Chrysler's driver seat. *Management Review, 83*(2), 30–32.
(Adapted)

as president of General Motors Europe from June 1988 until he left the company in March 1992 to join Chrysler as vice chairman and Iacocca's heir apparent.

Detroit-area writer Anita Pyzik Lienert interviewed Eaton at the automaker's headquarters in Highland Park, MI, to discuss management styles and the car industry.

Q.   How do you put your own managerial stamp on a sprawling organization such as Chrysler, especially after succeeding such a charismatic leader as Lee Iacocca?

Eaton: Lee Iacocca and I are as different as two people could possibly be. He was a sales and marketing guy who had worldwide visibility, and I suspect it would be correct to say that he was the best known businessman in the world, period. I have a much different approach. I'm an engineer, a car guy, who tries to build teams, who tries to be part of the team, who doesn't try to stand out. [I don't] aspire to making commercials or to be a world business leader, and that's good because I couldn't even if I wanted to.

We're totally, completely different people. But I don't think I'll have any less impact on Chrysler than Lee Iacocca did. It'll just be dramatically different because I'll come at it from an inside, teamwork standpoint as opposed to the approach he had. Not to say that either one is better than the other, it's just that I couldn't do it the way he did, and he probably couldn't do it the way I can.

Q.   How do you make the organization your own?

Eaton: I learned 30 years ago that as an individual I couldn't do very much. But by building a team, getting everybody to understand and agree on where we wanted to go and then empowering people, you can accomplish a tremendous amount. As I started to [direct] small groups and so forth, I quickly learned that telling other people what to do wasn't the right approach. You are better off agreeing on what you are going to do and who is going to do what, than having everyone go and do their own thing, including me. I still feel that way.

Q.   What advice did Mr. Iacocca give you when you succeeded him?

Eaton: Lee and I have an extremely good relationship, and there's no question that he gave me pointers—things to look out for. We had lots of very good conversations. It was more of a transition kind of thing [than advice].

Q.   Do you consider him a mentor?

Eaton: No. Lee Iacocca hired me, along with the board of directors, there's no question about that, but until five months or so before I came here, I'd never met him before. I got a call saying, would you talk to Lee Iacocca? I said sure, not even knowing is what it was going to be about. I'd seen him walking through auto shows and various places, but I'd never once met him.

Q.   How much contact do you have? Does he attend board meetings?

Eaton: Yes, he does. We have a terrific relationship, couldn't possibly be better, and I really do mean that. If he has a question, he calls me. If I have a question, I call him. He couldn't be happier. I couldn't be happier.

Q.   You've had the unique advantage of being in key executive positions at two of the biggest automakers in the world. How do the management styles differ at General Motors and Chrysler?

Eaton: The culture, the environment, et cetera, at Chrysler is very, very similar to GM of Europe. It would have been a much bigger shock to go from GM of Europe to [GM headquarters on] West Grand Boulevard than from GM of Europe to Chrysler. There was, at the time that I came back, a dramatically different culture at GM. Very hierarchical, very structured, with lots of committees, staffs and bureaucracies and so forth. There was none of that in Europe and there's none of that here.

Q.   Is Chrysler a better personal fit for you?

Eaton: Yes, absolutely.

Q.   Has GM made overtures to get you back in the GM fold?

Eaton: Heavens, no. I wouldn't go. I wouldn't be interested. I mean that only in the best of senses. The fact is that Jack [Smith] and I have a very good relationship—not that we agree on everything. That relationship plus what is going on in the industry and Washington have made it easy to get the three [auto] companies working very closely together. I'm not sure without the changes that occurred that we would have ever had that happen.

Q.   Is it a quirk of history that the heads of the Big Three all have management experience in Europe?

Eaton: Yes, but it's probably the best thing that could happen. We have spent a considerable amount of time talking to this Administration about how things work in Europe and how they work much better as a cooperative kind of relationship as opposed to an adversarial relationship. This has been obvious to me for a long time.

Ten or 15 years ago, it occurred to me that the number one advantage that Japan had over the rest of the world is that management, the workforce and the government worked together as one team and shared about 95 percent of the objectives. They each had their own little piece that they were trying to do, but 95 percent of what they were trying to accomplish was common among the three of them, and that's where you got Japan Inc.

The European experience teaches you that. Over there you have extremely close relationships with the workforce and management; you have a close relationship with government and lots of commonalities of purpose. The governments of Europe are focused on two things: the economy and inflation. After the economy, the thing they focus most on is workplaces—they don't call them jobs, they call them workplaces. They try to build a strong bond with industry and try to do whatever they can to make industry competitive because that's the only way you add workplaces. They come to you and say, what can we do? Here, nobody's ever come to industry and asked, what can we do? Industry goes to Washington and begs, could you help us by doing this?

Q.   Is that the kind of mentality you need to operate successfully in a global market?

Eaton: Sure. You'll be a lot more competitive if you're working together, as opposed to working as an adversary. I don't know of any adversarial relationship that produces the results you get by working together.

Q.   Is management style different among the Japanese?

Eaton: There are huge differences. There's as much difference in Japanese management as there is in American management. Clearly, the consensus approach dominates in Japan as opposed to a much more individual approach to management over here, but the extremes are no different. You find some real dictators in Japan.

Q. Do you prefer to work with one culture versus the other?

Eaton: Oh, [I prefer to work with] Europe. Japan is fairly difficult to work with only because the culture is dramatically different and the language is dramatically different. Let's face it, America came out of the European cultures. It's a melting pot of the European cultures. Asians came in after the overall culture in America was set.

Q. How did somebody who comes out of middle America learn to operate globally?

Eaton: It wasn't anything I was ever conscious of. I can tell you, without question, that the biggest growth experience of my life was the Europe assignment. Without that, I would not have been qualified to come here. I had been in operating jobs before, but never had a complete company. And frankly, GM Europe operates just about like an autonomous company. It doesn't share products. I used to always say one of the best things about working there was that it was 6,000 miles from Detroit.

Q. Does the chief executive of an American multinational company have to have overseas operating experience to broaden his or her perspective?

Eaton: Obviously not, because most of them don't. But it's a tremendous plus. We've talked within Chrysler, and we think that you ought to get some [overseas] experience for people because it's far more broadening than anything you could possibly do in a different assignment domestically.

Q. When sourcing vehicles and components in Mexico, how do you square things with your hourly workers in the United States?

Eaton: Chrysler has a $1.1 billion trade surplus, by year, with Mexico. Last calendar year, we added $250 million and we expect that to grow. There are 120 hours of total U.S. labor in a U.S. car built in the United States. A vehicle produced in Mexico, sent to the United States, has 70 hours of U.S. labor in it. A vehicle produced in Mexico for Mexico still has 50 hours of U.S. labor. Without NAFTA, we will have 4,000 jobs in the United States for stuff we're doing in Mexico. With NAFTA, it'll be 8,000.

Q.   What are you doing to get more women and minorities into key line positions?

Eaton: Chrysler actually has got a pretty darn good record. . . . I have to say we're making very good progress. You have to be very proactive. We don't actually set quotas, but we set targets. And then we do everything we can possibly do to get good people to fit. But you don't compromise your standards significantly to do it.

Q.   Is Chrysler doing anything specifically in the way of management training for women and minorities?

Eaton: We do more with women and minorities than we probably do with white males. That is one area that we've targeted as significant—that we need to significantly improve for everybody.

It does take time. Generally in the auto business, with a few exceptions, people come in out of college and stay. There's not a lot of movement between companies; there's not a lot of people brought in at high levels. I don't know the number of people that we're bringing in now, but in the technical areas I would suspect that women and minorities together probably [make up] 35 percent to 40 percent. It's very high. Ten years ago, it was about 25 percent.

Q.   What is your definition of a leader, especially as businesses get ready to enter a new century? What is your definition of a manager?

Eaton: I don't want any managers. Period. I only want leaders. Managers sit back and direct. Leaders get involved and show the way.

Q.   Mr. Iacocca is virtually assured a place in history as a sort of American folk hero. How will business history remember Robert Eaton?

Eaton: It probably won't. It will know that Chrysler is the premier car company in the world.

Discussion Questions

1. Compare the full range of leadership styles of Robert J. Eaton and former Chrysler chairman Lee Iacocca. Describe each leader's strengths and weaknesses.
2. Why do you think Iacocca selected Eaton to succeed him?
3. What recommendations do you have for Mr. Eaton, to improve his leadership style?
4. What are some of the challenges for a leader who succeeds someone like Lee Iacocca, who was a charismatic leader and public hero?

8

Turnaround Drama
Instills Leadership*

The Aluminum Company of America's (ALCOA) Magnesium Plant in Addy, Washington, was in trouble in 1989. Serious injury rates were high at 12.8 per year, and the plant was rocked by its first ever fatality. Its management structure accounted for most of Addy's troubles. National management stepped in and replaced the plant manager with Don Simonic. Simonic displayed the kind of authority that many had observed lacking at Addy. In setting goals for the plant, Simonic sought input from top-level management, made the decisions about goals, and avoided getting bogged down in the consensus problems that had paralyzed the plant. According to then-personnel manager Tom McCombs, Simonic was guided by four clear principles: Leaders have to lead, leaders have to make decisions, leaders have to have a clear vision, and leaders have to set direction.

Every now and then a company's big turnaround reads like a staged drama. This is especially true when the drama involves life-and-death decisions involving people's jobs and safety. The Aluminum Company of America (ALCOA) story focuses on dramatic improvements in safety, productivity, and profitability as a result of a change in how authority was structured.

The setting is Alcoa's Industrial Magnesium Plant in Addy, Washington. The dramatis personae include the plant manager, consultants, personnel manager, and the hourly workers—100 of whom were about to lose their jobs. The scene takes place in 1989.

The Addy plant was in almost total disarray. Serious injury rates were high at 12.8 per year, and the plant was rocked by its first ever fatality.

---

*Olberding, S. (1998). Turnaround drama instills leadership. *Journal for Quality & Participation, 21*(1), 52–55. (Adapted)

Prices of magnesium dropped at the plant, selling for $1.45 at a cost of $1.48 to make. Quality control was below what was needed to counteract market forces, as magnesium recovery was at 72 percent of the raw material. But the death of an employee caused the most crushing blow.

"The fatality was devastating," says then-personnel manager, Tom Mc-Combs. "It looked like the leadership was not working. Seven Addy employees were related to the man who died." Safety had been a top priority at ALCOA ever since Chairman and CEO Paul O'Neill had come on board. "The plant had been losing money for about five years, but with the accident, O'Neill said Addy was losing on both fronts. If it didn't get turned around, he would close the plant. In fact, at the time, they were trying to sell it anyway," remarks McCombs. National management stepped in and replaced the plant manager.

Enter Don Simonic, the new plant manager. McCombs describes Simonic as a decisive leader whom people respected. Simonic had coaching experience in college football (McCombs recalls that Simonic was even asked to coach the Baltimore Colts once but went to serve in the armed forces in Korea instead) and would use these coaching skills to drive through necessary changes at Addy. "His kind of coaching was: if someone isn't doing his or her job, then you put that person on the bench. There is authority embodied in that but also a sense of being connected to his people," states McCombs. And, just like in football, some of the players got thrown out of the game. "He had some really tough calls to make, but he didn't hesitate to replace leaders where it was needed." Though McCombs already implemented change with the help of consultants, Robert and Patricia Crosby, at least six months before Simonic arrived, it was Simonic who displayed the kind of authority that many had observed lacking (or nearly nonexistent) at Addy. Together, McCombs, the Crosbys, and now Simonic planned the turnaround.

Their task, however, was daunting. Market forces continued to drive costs higher, productivity was flat, at best—employees complained about the lack of accountability, poor quality control, and inadequate leadership. "The whole organization had a very low morale," explains McCombs. "There was a crying out for leadership."

Alcoa was far from being a bastion of traditional, hierarchical management. On the contrary, it had a team-based culture and what was considered a revolutionary management approach called "open systems," which was adapted from socio-technical systems theory. The business press even heralded ALCOA as a model plant in the tradition of the Procter & Gamble soap plant.

Inside and outside ALCOA, Addy wasn't perceived as just any plant. Built in 1975, it supplied ALCOA with magnesium alloy used in manufacturing aluminum. It was unique in that it used an experimental French magnesium technology, as well as the newer organizational design. The autonomous or self-directed work teams structure lacked immediate supervisors and featured "flexible work," where a team managed their own work area. This work team structure was touted as a first for heavy industry, and visitors flocked to the plant well through the mid-[19]80s to review the plant for themselves.

In practice, however, the management structure accounted for most of Addy's troubles. "Without clear authority, no one is empowered," according to Robert Crosby. And in his book, *Walking the Empowerment Tightrope: Balancing Management Authority and Employee Influence* (Organization Design and Development, Inc., 1992), Crosby writes, "A major problem in organizations is the exercise of either too much management authority and power, or the other extreme, abdication. Empowerment programs are falsely aimed at hourlies and as such are doomed to go the way of other fads and slogans. Authority must be balanced."

At ALCOA there appeared to be what the consultants called an "authority vacuum." McCombs explains that in a traditional plant, "we would've worked to get the supervisors to back off, whereas here, we needed to help them step up and make tough decisions." Illustrating how dissatisfied the teams were, McCombs remembers, "When Simonic went around to interview the teams, one guy came up and said 'Why doesn't ALCOA just put foremen back? We don't have any accountability left.' "

The problematic empowerment model exercised at Addy before the change process began featured an hourly leadership in which team coordinators were elected about every one to two years. Other hourly leadership positions consisted of a safety person, a training person, and someone called a "team resource," who was similar to an internal facilitator.

Additionally, supervisors, called "shift coordinators," had as many as four or five teams reporting to them, so they were connected to the team coordinators in some way. "We discovered, however, that we had a problem because the [shift coordinators] did not want to 'invade' the teams. So they kept staying hands off because if they did intervene, they would get in trouble because the teams would say, 'Leave us alone. We know what we're doing.' And if they didn't intervene, upper management would say that the teams weren't doing what they should be. So they were caught in the middle," explains McCombs. Eventually management had to take over some of the teams.

McCombs cites a lack of clarity in decision-making and authority as the main culprit in this empowered but troubled environment. To restore clarity, the first step of the Crosby plan focused on the new plant manager becoming clearer about goals. In setting these goals for the plant, Simonic did something very different from what any previous plant manager had done. According to the Crosbys, "Although he sought input from top-level management, he made the decisions about goals and avoided getting bogged down in the consensus problems that had paralyzed the plant."

As the turnaround proceeded, Simonic decided that cutting staff would be essential to meeting the new goals. First, all temporary and contract workers were laid off and next, in the very meeting where Simonic was to announce a further layoff of 100 hourly workers—roughly eight per team—the climax of the Addy drama took place.

As leaders were explaining the facts that had led to Simonic's decision, an hourly worker stood and spoke. He related a breakthrough his team had made in significantly reducing the downtime required to turn a furnace around. This process involved switching over to a new crucible once the other was filled. (McCombs compares this process to the manufacturing SMED single minute exchange of dyes-breakthrough process.)

"Simonic quickly calculated the proposed savings and said, 'If you can show the other teams how to do that in the next two weeks, then we won't have a layoff,' " McCombs remembers. Since each minute of downtime cost the company about $32, this breakthrough team implemented a new process where eight, instead of two, employees did the work, completing the process significantly faster. They reduced the usual one and-a-half-hour turnaround time to just one hour. Simonic called off the impending layoffs. When the new process was implemented on all nine furnaces in the plant, the savings reached $10 million—more than the wages of the 100 employees who kept their jobs.

The next big task for Addy players was to hold strategic meetings to align all parts of the system, clarify who would be making what decisions, explain how decisions could be influenced, and communicate why decisions were made. Simonic engaged both salaried and non-salaried employees in intensive dialogue. Then he set the goals. McCombs remembers how they developed a matrix reflecting what kind of decisions both team members and supervisors would make. They stipulated that the supervisors would still retain authority over all of them if they needed to. Since decisions at the plant before Simonic's arrival had been made largely by consensus, Simonic talked to all employees plant-wide in small groups.

Simonic made clear statements like, "These are the goals. You and all our employees have firsthand knowledge of how things work around here. I don't care how you get there. I will support you in making choices about how to get there. And, if you can't get there, I will step in and decide how we will get there."

As a result of this process, one person was made responsible for every project or task, also known as single-point accountability (SPA). This was a big change from how the plant had originally been set up, where, according to Crosby, consensus was "enshrined."

"The accepted notion throughout the plant had been that if we gave the team accountability, they would handle the [entire] project. Well, that didn't work very well," admits McCombs. With single-point accountability, "You know who is going to do what for which kinds of projects," says McCombs.

For that kind of accountability to succeed, McCombs believes you need to establish the "by whens"—in other words, when will the particular task get accomplished, noting the time on a certain day. For both the teams and employees it was now "clear what we expected, and they started achieving goals better," McCombs adds.

Eighteen months after ALCOA's national leaders began conversations with the soon-to-be-displaced plant manager, the bulk of the change efforts had been completed. Although positive signs had appeared throughout the process, the incident in which the layoffs were averted proved to be the most critical. Because employees had taken responsibility for applying their own creativity to meeting the overall goals, impressive results were achieved: costs had been reduced from $1.48 to $1.18, recovery of magnesium increased by 5 percentage points (worth $1.3 million per point), and the serious-injury frequency rate fell from 12.8 to 6.3 per year.

The plant kept breaking records for the next two years, going so far as to become the lowest-cost producer in the world. By 1993 the plant had boosted productivity by 72 percent ("The Technology Payoff," *Business Week*, June 14, 1993). The president of ALCOA even asked all of the plant managers to visit the site and learn from the Addy turnaround.

Unfortunately Addy didn't sustain the momentum of the turnaround. In 1992, Simonic and McCombs left Addy and went on to the challenge of turning around other ALCOA plants. "The upward spiral had lasted about four years and even though [Addy] experienced more breakthroughs in technology, more profit, and more improvements in what we had built, they didn't pay attention to the floor," reflects McCombs. "ALCOA started doing some studies and really reduced external head count. They eliminated all the department heads that were in that plant and everybody was basically reporting to the shift supervisor or plant manager. It caused unclarity about leadership and authority in decision-making all over again," explains McCombs. "They stripped away the leadership that could have supported the change efforts afterwards."

McCombs further believes that after he and Simonic left, Addy had neglected to perform the support work, details, or "maintenance tasks," as he refers to them. "We did a lot of work. We had nine internal people devoted to supporting the change effort; half hourly and half salaried trained at Addy, so the internal facilitator could do a lot of feedback work, transitioning, and other 'OD stuff' when new leaders came in. But when we left, they stopped doing it. They didn't think they needed it anymore," McCombs laments. McCombs has since learned not to rely on the momentum that accompanies a turnaround. Instead of looking for the next best practice or program, he says you should continue to maintain the actions that made you successful.

Currently, the plant is back on track and appears headed for success again. Perhaps because of the previous successes and the skills gained in the previous turnaround, the Crosbys believe the recovery currently underway is going to be much easier.

Of the lessons learned through the turnaround, the players of the Addy drama convey the need for constancy in decision-making and accountability. One decision-making technique that's now practiced at Addy and several other ALCOA plants is consultative decision-making, where the "boss" makes the final decision but consults with the team first. For example, McCombs recalls an incident requiring disciplinary action on several teams. "The teams would have 24 hours to give their recommendations to management on how the discipline should be handled—up to and including termination—and management would administer the discipline. At least 95 percent of the time we took the team's recommendation and moved on," says McCombs.

The teams also assist with hiring decisions using the consultative method. For example, the boundaries laid out for a team may concern ALCOA's desire to hire minorities. Typically, "The team would present their selection of whom to hire to the manager, and often they would do such a good job the decision was just 'rubber-stamped,' " explains McCombs.

Another successful approach was one Crosby developed called the "cadre." During the turnaround, Simonic and Crosby would work with the cadre, a group of key people, chosen from a vertical slice of the employees, who engaged in two specific roles: (1) observing and evaluating the change process as it plays out while (2) simultaneously participating in the process. The cadre became a skilled resource for the plant on leadership development, change management, conflict management, quality, and work processes.

In assessing if a turnaround drama like the one at Addy has to have a leader like Simonic, McCombs concedes that Simonic became the main character at Addy. He believes, however, that other processes must be in place for a turnaround momentum to be maintained. "Don had a dynamic personality and was very charismatic. He possessed a very strong leadership style and was very clear," McCombs says. "But you also must work with the intact families in the organization—one of Simonic's own beliefs. That's where change happens—in the small groups. You must work with that supervisor and that crew and get them aligned with the organization and work out any conflict. It's a lot harder, but that's what you have to do to maintain a success story like Addy."

The impact of Simonic's leadership on the employees seems indisputable. "Employees even called him 'Addy Moses,'" McCombs recalls. "He boosted their sense of security." According to McCombs, Simonic was guided by four clear principles. "Leaders have to lead, make decisions, have a clear vision, and set direction. Once leaders set direction and get a breakthrough goal in mind that people can rally around, then people can tell the leader how they are going to get it done. A leader shouldn't tell how to do it, but he or she needs to set that direction. And that's what Simonic did very well," insists McCombs.

Discussion Questions

1. Describe Simonic's full range of leadership style and how it made empowerment work at Addy.
2. What could Simonic, McCombs, and national management have done to keep their reforms in place after McCombs and Simonic were transferred?
3. Can you give some examples of the components of tranformational and transactional leadership in Simonic's and McCombs' behavior?
4. What did you personally like most about their leadership styles? Least? Why?

CHAPTER

9

Leading Ladies*

Local politics were the building blocks that helped shape both Fran Wilde's leadership of Tradenz (Trade New Zealand) and her directorship skills. Her strengths are being open and able to communicate. She made sure that she was available to address issues of a major political party in New Zealand. Formerly a Labour cabinet minister and Wellington mayor, Fran Wilde is CEO of Tradenz, a director of ANZ Banking Group (NZ) and Brierley Investments, chair of the Wellington Stadium Development Trust, and member of the Project K Trust Board. She formerly chaired Housing New Zealand, Community Housing, Victoria Link, and was a director of Tourism Wellington. Vicki Buck was a leader and enjoyed leadership with laughter. She wants people to like their work and feel passionate about it. She sees her "role as team manager, to empower a creative thinking system to turn institutionalized bureaucracy on its head."

There's a fresh force in the boardroom, a new breed of director leading the way as we barrel towards the next millennium, professional women who're smart, sharp and sought after.... Thousands of words will be written about two women this year, as New Zealand comes to grips with the women leading our two major political parties.

Fran Wilde

The rough and tumble of central and local politics were the building blocks that helped shape Fran Wilde's leadership and directorship skills.

---

*Tapsell, S. (1998). Leading ladies. *Management—Auckland, 45*(1), 24–37. (Adapted)

The helicopter view of running the country, and the more focused role of running Wellington were dynamic ingredients for her role as Tradenz (Trade New Zealand) boss when she took the job last year.

Wilde moved into the public arena in 1981 after winning the Wellington Central seat for Labour. When Labour came to office in 1984 until 1990, she was Government Whip, Minister of Tourism, Minister of Disarmament and Associate Minister of Foreign Affairs and Trade.

But biding her time in the opposition benches was not for the energetic Wilde. She left Parliament in 1992, winning the Wellington mayoralty. "I left in the middle of a term for a number of reasons, but I have to say, like virtually all politicians, I felt being in Opposition wasn't much chop. The Wellington mayoralty was an opportunity to focus on issues with which I was familiar, and on which I'd worked as an MP. It was also a chance to try out what I considered to be a new style of leadership. I went from Parliament, which was extremely hierarchical, divisive, combative, into a council which had been divided along local political lines."

Her challenge was to weld the group together for a common good—the good of Wellington. "It was a major challenge for me, I said 'let's try and work on the issues and not speak through party mouthpieces all the time.' It was a huge change for Wellington and I believe it was a healthy one, a positive one and well received by the people."

The "Positively Wellington" campaign is part of her legacy. The campaign showed Wellingtonians they lived in a great place, and told the rest of the country to visit.

Wilde's a great believer in leaders doing their own SWOT analysis. "You need to know yourself well. To be conscious of your own style and its impàct on others. I know I'm very over the top, I'm very overtly up front and of course there can be dangers in that. I've been told that thinking aloud can be difficult for some who can't cope with a leader who has this style," she smiles.

However, being open and communicative are her strengths. "And a sense of purpose or vision, if you want to call it that . . . they're both appropriate for public and organisational leadership." A company won't prosper unless it has good leadership. It may do short term, but long term it won't because the team won't work together. "So in the public, my leadership role was one of having the vision, articulating it, of being open, being available, which means you're very busy."

Within five months of being at the Tradenz helm, Wilde had already made changes. The most obvious changes are the physical ones. Not content to preach openness, she pulled down office walls to prove it. "We're now completely an open plan organisation, which is all part of encouraging more flexibility in our work patterns. Remote leadership doesn't work in my book. Demagogues come to a sticky end. You can't run an organization from a mobile phone. You've got to be there." Corridor talk is important. "The discussion you have with someone when you bump into them is the most effective way of moving things on."

Vicki Buck

[Vicki Buck has been] mayor of Christchurch since 1989, and a director of Christchurch City Holdings, Trustbank Canterbury Community Trust, Canterbury Development Corporation and the Christchurch College of English Language.

Leadership with laughter is high on the list of Christchurch Mayor Vicki Buck. "I think people work better together when they're enjoying themselves. I'd rather people cracked a few jokes and had a good time, otherwise meetings could be very long. For most of our council meetings it's sometimes hard to know who's on which party, there's often too much laughter," says Buck, laughing of course. "If you're not enjoying it you shouldn't be doing it is my rationale for being mayor. Plus the idea that I wanted to make Christchurch different. I grew up in Christchurch, and I think it was a boring city to have grown up in. I think being a boring city is an unforgivable sin. So I didn't want the city I felt passionately about to be classed as boring."

Determined to make a difference, Buck was elected to the Christchurch City Council when she was 19 years old, while she was studying local government finance for her MA degree. She then moved into social work and business research where she helped set up economic development initiatives, and council marketing promotions.

The mayoralty gave her the opportunity to be in charge of the social change she feels passionate about in the city. "I like the big picture. For instance, I can't get passionate about the details of roads and sewerage, we have staff who understand those details. Although I have learned [these details] along the way, generally I'm happy to delegate that kind of detail."

"That's why the social area is more satisfying," she says. "Take the challenge of how to make the city friendly for children. There's no engineering solution or formula for that. So these areas are more demanding because you don't know the right answer, often you're making it up as you go along." It's in these areas that Buck has made her mark on the city. "Within council I encourage people to initiate new ideas; things like helping the community fund their own ideas, and use their own networks."

The [19]90s have seen results. The growth of the city's cafe and bar scene pleases her, as well as Christchurch's reputation as an international tourism spot. "I like events that reach out to lots of people." "Kidsfest," a nine-day winter event aimed at 2–12 year olds, was established six years ago for example. "It started small, and is now very successful," says Buck.

She also initiated the "Festival of Romance," held 10 days before Valentine's Day, and the Canterbury Adventure Festival, a 10-day adventure festival promoting Canterbury as an outdoor/thrill-seeker destination. "They're often small things in themselves but they add up." She's aware she's sometimes criticized for looking at the big picture, but is quick to add she knows when to look at the detail. "If it involves commitment of council resources for instance, I get involved in the detail. During budget week I'll always sit through the entire council budget decisions, because that's where you make decisions that drive what you can do for the next year. But I do like to experiment. To have a go. Get council to take risks and make mistakes and be prepared to look at things as a research and development exercise."

"Rather than the concept that things must be in perfect order before you go ahead, [Buck says] I don't think you need to research to death to the point where you miss an opportunity." Successful organizations of the future will be those that think on their feet, and those whose leaders foster creative thinking, she believes. "I'd like to eventually think council was an organization that embodied creative thinking. That might sound like a contradiction in terms, but I don't think it needs to be. I see my role as team manager, to empower a creative thinking system, to turn institutionalized bureaucracy on its head. The difficulty with politics is that you always get adversarial thinking. You get brownie points for smart thinking against an idea rather than exploring the concepts behind it, or moving forward together. I like the concept of 'of course you can,' to be told by a big institution you can have a go and see if you can do it."

Discussion Questions

1. How does the context affect the success of these female leaders' styles of leadership?
2. What is the best aspect of each of their styles of leadership?
3. How do their styles of leadership differ from those of more traditional male politicians?
4. Do you think that humor should be considered an aspect of a leader's style? Why?

10

The Many Facets
of Tina's Leadership*

Effective leadership is not limited to heads of organizations or to one best way. We found a head tour manager, Tina, who exemplified an effective leader. Tina was responsible for conducting a study group of 30 across Sicily for 2 weeks.

The 30 started mainly as strangers to each other and ranged in age from 40 to 80 years. The places to be visited were set in advance, but to suit the needs of the group Tina used considerable discretion in deciding the order of activities during any given day and added unexpected little diversions. But before deciding on the itinerary for any particular day, she always consulted the group to check for agreement on the plans and/or changes for the day (although not the times or order, which depended on whether and when sites were open). Because the overall program for each day was set in advance, she provided full information by posting times and places in advance of each day as well as announcing them at dinner the night before. In addition to detailing the day's schedule, she also gave useful background information on what was going to be available at different locations to handle the variety of needs that would arise during each day among the group. As she knew the travel times and requirements to match visiting times with the hours that museums, churches, temples, archeological sites, pubs, and restaurants were open, she was firm in setting the very early wake-up calls and early starts, even though it often meant six or fewer hours of sleep. Tina set a high standard of on-time departures, not by any punitive action

---

*An original case written by the editors.

such as leaving a tardy participant behind, but instead by showing her continuing caring and concern for each and every member of the group.

Aside from wanting to conform, we wanted to be "on time" for early morning departures or when returning to the bus after a free hour of strolling in a village, to show support for Tina's exceptional efforts to help each and every one of us with any sort of problem. She was always ready to suggest alternative ways out of dilemmas. Whatever happened, Tina remained kind, considerate, and able to cope effectively with stressful events. When one of our elderly passengers slipped and broke her elbow, Tina personally took charge and arranged for quick medical attention and assistance, somehow managing to keep everything running smoothly and on schedule for the rest of the group.

Thus, on the one hand, she was firm in giving direction, as legitimate for her role; on the other hand, she was friendly, caring, personal, and considerate. For the mainly routinized nature of her tasks and goals, she initiated many of the needed arrangements while demonstrating a great deal of concern for our well being. Like the best of leaders with such programmed responsibilities, she was strong in both *initiation* and *consideration*. Also, she worked in excellent coordination with her colleagues: an historian who accompanied us and the required local tour guides. The group was extremely satisfied with Tina and her leadership. Furthermore, we felt that the goals of the study group were fully achieved.

Tina actually showed much more in her leadership—what we now have come to see as *transformational leadership*. Her behavior and influence were idealized. The 30 members in our group identified with Tina's aims to create a highly satisfactory set of experiences for us. She demonstrated a high level of professionalism and was a role model for our group. She was *inspirational* in the way she expressed herself. She often used colorful metaphors to increase the appeal of what we were about to see. Not only was she able to create satisfactory alternatives when necessary, she was *intellectually stimulating*. How? She encouraged others in the group to create options and alternatives by accepting innovative suggestions from them and then proceeding to put those suggestions into effect. She was *individually considerate*. For instance, a group member might want to spend more time in a particular location. Tina would make suitable arrangements for that one member with a complete absence of annoyance and hassle. Or she might check with the whole group to see if it wanted to spend more time in a spot than originally scheduled. Tina exhibited transformational leadership, and did so in a temporary role as a leader in a temporary group.

But leadership is not always so effective and satisfying in the long run to those who follow some seemingly transformational leaders. *Pseudotransformational* leaders do much of the same things as do transformational leaders. However, they are like the Pied Piper of Hamlin and lead their groups for the leaders' own personal satisfaction, not to meet the true needs, aims, and goals of those they seduce into following them.

When looking at leaders and leadership, it is important to acknowledge that leadership may be attempted, succeed or fail, and be effective or ineffective. Tina *attempted* leadership, which often *succeeded.* Followers were influenced in the directions desired by her. She frequently told us where and when to reassemble after being free to wander and we were almost always at the reassembly point at the time she indicated. But sometimes Tina's attempted leadership failed. For instance, several times Tina suggested that her group eat in a particular restaurant, but most of us rejected her suggestion. When this occurred, she was open to alternative suggestions and worked with the group to come up with an acceptable solution.

As we have said, initiation and consideration exemplify the traditional but limited way of conceptualizing leaders. Transformational leaders will engage in either or both when they are acting as transactional leaders. Instead of moving those led to go beyond their self-interests, transactional leaders cater to the self-interests of those whom they influence. They offer inducements for their followers to move in the direction desired by the leader that also meet the self-interests of the followers. They exchange promises of reward for cooperation and compliance of their followers. Such transactions are constructive and usually are reasonably effective. Alternatively, the transactional leaders may actively or passively engage in corrective transactions. Here the exchange is change in behavior, learning, cooperation, or compliance of followers to avoid censorship, reproof, negative feedback, punishment, or disciplinary action. Both constructive and corrective transactions are contingent on the followers' performance. Some leaders emphasize constructive promise, praise, and reward contingent on good performance. Other leaders manage by exception and pay attention to their followers only when their performance is off the mark and correction is needed. Although constructive transactions are reasonably successful and effective, corrective transactions are less so. In all, transactional leadership is not enough. People are not always responsive if treated exclusively like commodities that can be moved forward with the enticement of a carrot or the threat of a stick.

When leadership is needed, any leadership at all is likely to be more successful and effective than avoidance of the responsibility to provide leadership. Laissez-faire leadership is the behavior of those individuals in a group who don't care what happens, avoid taking responsibility, cannot make up their minds, and are satisfied to sit and wait for others to take the necessary initiatives imposed by the tasks at hand.

Think about the last time you were confronted with a choice of sitting back and waiting for someone else in your group to say what was needed to be said for the group to move forward, or taking the initiative yourself.

Were you reluctant to act? If so, why? What made you finally do what you did? Was it leadership?

Discussion Questions

1. Identify what you consider to be Tina's greatest strength as a leader.
2. How committed would you be to working with Tina? Why?
3. How would you improve on Tina's leadership style?
4. Was there any pseudotransformational leadership in Tina's performance as a tour leader?

II

LEADER DEVELOPMENT
AND SUCCESSION

Part II deals with lessons on what factors develop leaders and how experiences shape their subsequent performance. Special attention is paid to women leaders whose career paths have moved them into top management positions. The cases in Part II are as follows:

11. Playing Powell Politics
12. Larry Bossidy
13. Gertrude Boyle
14. A. Diane Moeller: A Talk With the Healthcare Forum's Incoming Chair
15. Leadership of Renewal: Leadership for the 21st Century
16. Profiles of Two Successful Women Managers
17. Nimrod Press

11

Playing Powell Politics*

General Colin Powell's success can be attributed to a great deal of hard work. Perhaps his most noteworthy characteristics are humor and self-confidence. His natural talent for leadership was developed by his experience in the Army.

A Favorable Background

Powell's life story, impressive as it is, is not a tale of struggle against adversity. Born into a strong middle-class family of Jamaican immigrants, growing up in a relatively safe and cohesive multiethnic neighborhood in the Bronx, Powell attended City College when its standards were still high. He came from a social stratum that supplied, and still supplies, the military with most of its leaders. He entered the U.S. Army at just the point when the color of his skin was no bar to advancement—if anything, as he tacitly admits, rather the reverse. He encountered formal, overt racial discrimination in its last days in the South, but off military bases, not on them. A natural soldier who loved his trade, he did well at each level of command and had opportunities for professional advancement and further education offered to him by an institution that also provided the company of comrades. At no stage in his career did he lack exemplars and patrons who thought well of him and advanced his career accordingly. His private life, one readily sees, has been blessed by an exceptionally strong marriage and family life, the support of a devout Episcopalian faith, and a ready capacity for friendship.

---

*Cohen, E. A. (1995). Playing Powell politics—*My American Journey* by Colin Powell. *Foreign Affairs, 74*(6), 102–110. (Adapted)

Colin Powell did not claw his way to the top in the face of professional or personal hardship; he rose in favorable circumstances by ability and ebullient charm.

None of this detracts from Powell's virtues, which even in a co-authored, carefully drafted book of this kind [Powell's autobiography *My American Journey*, written before he became Secretary of State] shine through. His robust sense of the absurd manifests itself in anecdotes told at his own expense. It is difficult to contrive humor, and its continual presence in the book, as in personal encounters with Powell, reflects something essential about the man. More than once Powell refers to his hot temper, and one suspects that his ability to guffaw has neutralized the acid in an anger that, he admits, periodically erupted in shouting at subordinates. Humor bespeaks as well a sense of proportion; it fits with the self-portrait of a man who as a commander wasted little time with the more senseless forms of spit and polish, who tried to wrap up work by 5:30 P.M., and who enjoyed a good party. Indeed, more than once Powell wistfully recalls the days when the army did not regard a drink too many as grounds for the termination of a career. Humor and self-confidence often go together, and the latter characteristic is even more notable than the former. On the night following tense interviews for the White House Fellows program, Powell was partying while his competitors nervously waited for envelopes to be slipped under their doors at Airlie House.

[Showing a] disdain for deep thinkers, Powell often repeats the injunction, "Don't trust the experts," a sentiment that reflects not merely mistrust of others but confidence in himself. He describes his rethinking of the American defense posture in 1994 as a back-of-the-envelope exercise: "What I was hatching amounted to analysis by instinct. I was not going on intelligence estimates, war games, or computer projections." This self-confidence leads to Powell's third great asset, a natural talent for leadership, developed by the army through simple maxims that all second lieutenants learn but not all take to heart: "Take care of your people," "The boss eats last," and the like. Many of these are included in the book as "Colin Powell's Rules," 13 maxims ("Check small things," "Don't take counsel of your fears or naysayers") that are sound advice if not necessarily profound truths.

In truth Powell's career beginnings were those of a foot soldier. Powell's fundamental outlook on military matters—including his disdain for "deep thinkers," "intelligence wizards," and "puffed-up pilots"—are those of the bred-in-the-bones infantryman. His early training and posts—the army's grueling Ranger program, a plum instructorship at the infantry school at Fort Benning, command of a brigade in the elite 101st Airborne Division—bespeak a talent for genuine soldiering. Equally revealing is his admiring discussion of his division commander in 1973–74, Major General Hank "Gunfighter" Emerson, a study in leadership under difficult circumstances, of an

army inundated with misfits and troublemakers but determined to pull itself out of its Vietnam trough.

Discussion Questions

1. How important is a sense of humor to leading?
2. Do you agree with Powell's injunction "Don't trust the experts"? Does
   Powell's injunction reflect a confidence in himself?
3. Could Powell have risen as high as he did without a good sense of
   humor?
4. How would you improve Powell's style of leadership?

12

Larry Bossidy*

Six U.S. executives who once worked for John F. Welch, Jr., General Electric Company's near-legendary chairman and CEO, are now putting their considerable talents to work at their own companies. Although GE and Welch can be credited for uniquely developing these superstars, it cannot be assumed that they are Welch copycats. One of these executives is Lawrence A. Bossidy, chairman and CEO of Allied Signal Corporation. Some advice from Bossidy includes implement an honest appraisal system, be humble and ready to listen, and increase communication between layers of the organization.

Six U.S. executives who once worked for John F. Welch, Jr., near-legendary CEO, are now putting their considerable talents to work at their own companies. Credit GE and Welch for uniquely developing these superstars, but don't assume they're Welch copycats.

The exemplary group of six CEOs that GE has spun off during Welch's 16-year tenure as CEO includes Lawrence A. Bossidy. Former GE vice chairman Bossidy has been chairman and CEO of the $14-billion Allied Signal Corporation, Morristown, NJ, since mid-1991.

Honest Appraisal

Part of the change equation demands we let employees know how they're doing. That means management must learn to appraise employees in a constructive manner. Fortunately, more and more companies are realizing the

*McClenahen, J. S. *(1997, July 7). Jack's men. *Industry Week*, pp. 12–17. (Adapted)

importance of the evaluation process for both factory workers and professionals. The old practice of obfuscating appraisal forms is out the window. Middle managers were terrific at filling pages and saying nothing. Now we're more creditable: We tell people what their development needs are and help them overcome problems.

We now use different assessment forms that list attributes and development needs and detail an employee's likely career progression. Once people saw management was willing to help, there was a lot more buy-in.

Facets of Change

Knowing what he knows now, this is one aspect of change management [Bossidy] would treat differently.

Bossidy [explains], "We flooded employees with initiatives. We overdid it. I think we should have paced ourselves more. The problem was that I had my priorities, and the people working for me had theirs, and it cascaded. The poor people who were trying to field all of these things became overwhelmed and disillusioned. We had to make a mid-course correction."

[Of] the change insight or process which was most useful to him and the change practice he learned from because it failed, Bossidy says: "The most useful thing I've learned is to be humble and listen. The most significant failure results from trying to orchestrate change with layer upon layer of organization. If you don't reduce the layers and improve the communication up and down the change chain, you have no chance."

BLEEDING ARM, BUT NO BLEEDING HEART*

It seems uncharacteristic of Allied Signal's Larry Bossidy. Why is he hanging on to a dog of a business?

This is the kind of story they tell about the man: In October 1996, Bossidy, rushing to get to a meeting, slipped and fell in a Paris hotel room, opening a gash in his arm. He grabbed a hand towel for a tourniquet. With the bleeding stanched, he conducted the meeting without anyone being aware he was hurt. On the company jet en route to another appointment, one of Bossidy's senior vice presidents called ahead for help. A country doctor at the rural airport in Waterford, Ireland, stitched up the grimacing Bossidy without anesthesia. Off he went to tour the company's nearby turbocharger plant. A guy like that doesn't waste a lot of sympathy on well-paid executives who don't deliver.

---

*Upbin, B. (1988, April 20). Bleeding arm, but no bleeding heart. *Forbes*, pp. 126–130.

Twice a year Allied Signal, Inc. Chairman Lawrence Bossidy summons 150 of his top managers to the company's Morristown, NJ, headquarters for a review. In a darkened auditorium he projects onto a wall what he calls the "leakers" list.

Since moving to head Allied in 1991, Bossidy has behaved very Welch-like. In 1996 he sold Allied's car braking division to Robert Bosch for $1.5 billion. Last November he also dumped the seat belts and air bag unit for $710 million.

Those two transactions lost approximately $3 billion in revenue. Automotive, once Allied's biggest item, is now third behind its much more profitable aerospace and chemicals groups.

Discussion Questions

1. How would you like to report directly to Bossidy? Why?
2. How would you feel being a lower-level manager in Bossidy's firm? Why?
3. How important are mentors to the development of leadership in organizations? How should such mentors be selected and developed?

13

Gertrude Boyle*

A generation ago and more, it was virtually unheard of for an American company to bring in an outsider to lead. However, as times have changed, market demands now shift more quickly and companies have to constantly reinvent themselves. In such a climate, a certain level of unfamiliarity with a new business can be an advantage.

In 1970, Gertrude Boyle's 47-year-old husband died of a heart attack, leaving her in charge of Columbia Sportswear. This Portland, OR, manufacturer of outdoor clothing was mortgaged to the hilt and within an inch of shutting down. Boyle's motto is "Early to bed, early to rise, work like hell, and advertise."

Who says it takes years of on-the-job experience to run a business? Sometimes an outsider's view is exactly what a company needs.

This is a story about amateurs. Not the kind of amateur whose golf handicap is 40. The kind of amateur who runs a $400 million company and while it is a word not often associated with CEO or chair, it is an accurate way to describe an executive who is suddenly thrown into an unfamiliar business and must learn and manage at the same time.

As in all things, not all amateurs are created equal. Some are recruited to the task. John Sculley, for example, who went from PepsiCo to Apple, or Gerald Greenwald of Chrysler and then United Airlines, or Louis Gerstner of RJR Nabisco and then IBM—and some get there by accident, as with several dozen women around the country who abruptly inherited large companies when their husbands died. All these outsiders face similar caveats and pit-

---

*Kaplan, J. (1997). Amateur's hour. *Working Woman, 22*(10), 28–33.

falls, but the more I researched the story—and particularly, the more I looked into the odyssey . . . of [a] remarkable [woman], Gertrude Boyle . . . the more I realized that the differences outweighed the similarities.

Probably the biggest difference between being recruited from a top job in another industry—moving essentially, from one exclusive club to another—and the serendipitous route is the cost of failure. These recruits weren't promised lifeboats or golden parachutes or any other easy means of escape from potential ruin. "What I always tell people," says Gertrude Boyle, "is that if someone asked you, 'Can you swim a mile?' you'd say, 'Nah.' But if you found yourself dumped out at sea, you'd swim the mile. You'd make it."

A generation ago and more, it was virtually unheard of for an American company to bring in an outsider to lead. In the '50s and '60s, after all, we were primarily a manufacturing economy, and corporations were rigidly hierarchical pyramids, the leaders invariably and perennially rising from the ranks. Too many jobs on a resume was a black mark to be explained away. "People used to put a higher value on loyalty and staying with one organization for a long time. It was thought to be one of the criteria for a successful career," says Linda Heagy, managing partner at the Chicago office of the executive-recruitment firm Heidrick & Struggles. "But as times have brought about market demands that shift more quickly, companies have had to constantly reinvent themselves, which often leaves them without the talent they need. Look at AT&T," she says. "It went from being a monopoly to being deregulated and thrown into a highly pitched battle for market share. It had never had to grow marketers before." Nor did it ever have to hire a CEO from outside, as it did last October, when it brought in John Walter of commercial printing company R. R. Donnelley & Sons, as the designated successor to chairman Robert Allen. Yet Walter ran into trouble from the jump, not only because of his unfamiliarity with the swiftly changing telecommunications business but also because his heir-apparent status prevented him from bringing along a support group of trusted executives from his previous company—the kind of support group that probably enabled Gerstner to survive and thrive at IBM.

A certain level of unfamiliarity with a new business isn't necessarily a problem; it can even be an advantage, says Joie Gregor, managing partner of Heidrick & Struggles's New York office. "When the company culture is so ingrained that it's really stalled, when there's a value system and everybody subscribes to it, creative thinking has also stalled," she says. "When somebody comes in from the outside, it can be very refreshing. They're going to ask questions, probe deeply." Thus Gerstner's very pertinent questions about IBM's plans to break up into smaller companies and about its identity as a monolithic producer of mainframes and PCs. By recasting Big

Blue as both a hardware manufacturer and a technological service provider, the canny outsider engineered a renaissance for the computer giant.

To be a successful outsider, Heagy says, requires a combination of business insight, vision, and sheer mettle. "You need the analytic skills to say, 'What is this balance sheet telling me?' And then you need the guts to cut away deadwood. It could be painful for a company to get out of the bread-and-butter, traditional parts of its business. But sometimes you have to be ruthless."

In 1970, Gertrude Boyle's 47-year-old husband, Neal, died of a heart attack. The housewife and mother, who by her own admission knew next to nothing about business, found herself in charge of Columbia Sportswear, a Portland, Oregon, manufacturer of outdoor clothing that was mortgaged to the hilt and within an inch of shutting its doors.

Her German-Jewish parents, who fled Europe in the 1930s with 13-year-old Gertrude in tow, founded Columbia and passed the company on to Neal Boyle; he was just getting it on its feet when he died. Longtime suppliers, afraid that a rank amateur (a woman to boot) wouldn't be able to run the company, refused to fill orders. The bank threatened to call in a crucial $180,000 loan Neal Boyle had taken out just before his death.

So the worried young widow asked her son, Tim, a journalism student at the University of Oregon, to help her run the company. Together they took charge, shakily. The first year after the novice management team was in place, Columbia's sales fell from $800,000 to $600,000. Deliveries were late, and debts mounted. Two years later, the company had run out of cash, and the bank refused to advance any more.

But when a potential buyer offered Boyle a bargain basement price, something in her snapped. She sent him scurrying with a barrage of choice language and put up the company's building as security for a bridge loan. She cut back on Columbia's wholesale operation, which was sponging cash, and trimmed its product lines to the bare bones.

She also had to trim personnel. "I had a horrible time when I first came in," Boyle says. "We had these women who did financial inventory. If I needed some numbers from them, they'd say, 'It's after 11:30; I'm busy.' Then the one in charge said she wasn't going to do inventory anymore unless I raised her salary. But she didn't know anything about female psychology. I let her stay one month, two months, while I learned how she did what she did. Then I said goodbye to her."

Boyle is a short, solid woman of 73 with a unique accent that combines German and northwestern tones, and a gimlet stare over multicolor-framed half-glasses. It's a famous stare. In 1993, Columbia's Portland-based ad agency, Borders, Perrin & Norrander, persuaded Boyle to become the figurehead for a nationwide print and TV campaign that portrayed her as

"One Tough Mother," a glowering drill sergeant of a corporate leader with a tattoo on her bicep that read Born to Nag. The campaign—along with the wildfire success of the Bugaboo parka, a jacket with a zip-out lining that can be worn separately—helped propel Columbia to just under $300 million in sales last year.

The advertising image, like most images, is strangely consonant with and divergent from reality. Boyle is tough—a sign in her office reads, "Old age and treachery will overcome youth and skill"—but with a good deal more of her own humor and warmth than the ads convey. She has the soul of an earthy hausfrau. "Early to bed, early to rise, work like hell, and advertise, that's my motto," she tells me, as we sit in her modest, windowless office in Columbia's headquarters. The in-basket on her desk is piled high with some two hundred checks for her to sign. Couldn't somebody else be doing this? Shouldn't the chief executive officer of Columbia be attending to the macro issues or be managing by walking around? The answer is that Boyle does plenty of both, and signing checks is just as important to her. For Boyle, micro and macro are much the same thing. "I like to know where my money is going," she says. "For instance, a guy who works here went out of town on business and put his car in the hourly lot at the airport. Now, we have a rule that we're all supposed to use economy parking. So when he submitted a bill for $75 for parking, I didn't pay it. Money doesn't grow on trees."

Her down-to-earth approach also applies to her relationship with her nine-hundred-plus employees, who seem more like an extended family than a work force. She knows most of their names, and they call her Gert. "The only people who call me Mrs. Boyle are the people at the front desk," she says, "and only because I don't like the way it sounds when they say, 'Hey, Gert! Get on the phone!' " It must be admitted, though, that her own style is more maternal than egalitarian. (One of her nicknames is Mother Boyle.) "Running a company is like raising kids," she says. "You all have to be in the same line of thinking."

At Columbia, it seems, they all are. The company's headquarters, in a big restored warehouse on a magnificent spot at a bend in the Willamette River, are clean, airy, and informal. There isn't a necktie or a high heel in sight, and most of the space is separated by low-rise dividers rather than walls. A piney north-woods scent pervades the oak- and brick-walled offices, and the workers seem exceptionally relaxed as Boyle inspects the premises. "I'll get those checks done today," she promises Marie in accounts payable.

It's an interesting way to run a $300 million company, and one that—just maybe—only a woman could have come up with. As we tool out in Boyle's red 1986 BMW convertible to inspect Columbia's warehouse facility, I ask whether the initial perception of her as a business outsider was ever a strategic advantage. "To some extent being a woman has helped, although you kind of have to elbow your way in. Guys don't like women to dictate. Even now at sales meetings, there's a little bit of hesitation when I say something. It's like, 'Are you sure?' But the publicity has helped. Phil Knight gets publicity because he's done well," she says of her friend and mentor, the CEO of nearby Nike. "I get publicity because I'm a woman."

Discussion Questions

1. To what full range of leadership factors do you attribute Gert Boyle's success?
2. If you were an employee of Columbia Sportswear, how would you feel about her mothering?
3. What would you recommend to enhance Boyle's style of leadership?
4. How will this company do once Gert Boyle is gone?

14

A. Diane Moeller: A Talk With the Healthcare Forum's Incoming Chair*

In the following case, A. Diane Moeller, the incoming chair of the Healthcare Forum and president and chief executive officer of Catholic Health Corporation (CHC), discusses leadership development in the healthcare industry, CHC's commitment to community service, what lies ahead for the Healthcare Forum, and the future for women in the healthcare industry. Moeller says that leadership development within the CHC starts with recruitment. She believes in promoting executives from within. The two attributes that healthcare leaders need in the 1990s are security and maturity. Whatever service CHC provides must be based on the needs of the community, not on the desires of the facility. The Healthcare Forum is interested in developing leaders who can integrate and apply to healthcare the best concepts from all kinds of organizations and industries. As organizations streamline, fewer positions will be available, and women may not have the opportunity to season themselves and grow. However, the management ranks are filled with young women coming up.

Whether Moeller is talking about leadership, community service, or visions for the future, what comes through is an impassioned and deeply value-oriented approach to her chosen work as both a healthcare leader and a guide to tomorrow's healthcare leaders. Indeed, The Healthcare Forum's incoming chair, A. Diane Moeller, knows a few things about leadership.

President and CEO of Catholic Health Corporation, her own track record as a leader is outstanding. Since she became CEO in 1987, Catholic Health Corporation has added to its system more than 10 new facilities and 2 religious orders. The corporation operates in 14 states and provides a continuum of services from tertiary care to housing for the elderly, as well as low-income housing at 104 sites. In 1990,

---

*Berger, S. (1991). Diane Moeller: A talk with the Healthcare Forum's incoming chair. *Healthcare Forum, 34*(3), 47–48. (Adapted)

Catholic Health Corporation's gross revenues topped $1 billion for the first time and its credit rating was A1A-plus.
Moeller has served on the board of the Healthcare Forum since 1987. Here are excerpts from our conversation with her:

"If I could do only one thing at CHC, it would be to develop leaders. The healthcare industry needs to have strong leaders, rather than politicians, plan its future. Leadership development within my own organization starts with recruitment. We work hard to ensure that we choose the right executive for the job. It's a difficult process, and there are no guarantees. (If I had a fool-proof method, I would sell it!)

"We try to get a sense of the individual, not just of his or her qualifications. When recruiting a healthcare facility CEO, we use a search committee, and have board and staff members interview the candidates. Ideally, we would visit the candidate's institution and speak with colleagues and acquaintances. We're exploring ways to be able to do that. I also believe in promoting executives from within. That's the best way to ensure consistency of values, to have a good feel for the person we're hiring for a job, and to reward people for performance.

"The two attributes healthcare leaders need . . . are *security* and *maturity*. They have to be secure enough to involve employees in decision-making and then trust them to do their jobs. And they have to be mature enough to put all their hopes and dreams on the table, and still realize they can't have it all.

"When you have secure, mature leaders, you can flatten your organization considerably. At CHC, few professionals report to a supervisor anymore, because the people who do the job are so closely involved in decision-making. Fostering that level of participation requires senior management to be secure and mature enough to handle the hard, gut-wrenching work of compromise and team problem-solving.

"Once I think I've hired the best person, my management philosophy is to trust that person to do the job. I know the choice was a good one if, about one year down the line, he or she can give me a good idea of what needs to be done, but also can admit to not knowing how to tackle every problem.

"I don't expect executives to know everything. If an institution has problems but the CEO is confident that they can be overcome and there is no instability in the workforce, I'm not going to get upset. But if someone tries to bluff me, then I'm worried."

Service First

"We've just completed our strategic plan at CHC. Our vision centers on the development of networks of services that embrace a continuum, of care. We will work with others, including Catholic and non-Catholic facilities and agencies outside our system, so that we can all better serve the communities that support us. This vision is not so unusual. Many healthcare organizations are realizing the importance of using strategic alliances to support growth. What sets us apart, I think, is our definition of community service: Whatever service we provide must be based on the needs of the community—not on the desires of the facility. It's like zero-based budgeting: We define our task in terms of what services we need to provide in order to improve a community's health and well-being. That's different from defining it only in terms of how to run a hospital or a nursing home most profitably. I'm the first to admit that such a value-based approach has tough economic and competitive implications. But healthcare leaders need to frame the issues differently: At CHC, for example, we ask 'Whom do we need to serve,' 'What will it take to serve them,' not 'What are the politicians going to do to us?' The bottom line at CHC is, if we can't integrate values, we can't be in service. If we found we could survive only if we stopped caring for poor people, then we would cease operations.

"Because Catholic healthcare probably is in its toughest time of transition, attention to values is especially important now. We have been dependent on the continuity of leadership of religious women. Now that there is a contraction in the healthcare ministry, the challenge to Catholic healthcare is to maintain its devotion to the values of the system, even though many of our leaders aren't members of religious orders, or even Catholic.

"We spend time with people in each institution and work with the local staff to help them understand how to live out values. We even teach them how to write out job descriptions based on those values."

What's Ahead for The Forum?

"The Healthcare Forum understands that leadership is not so much managing what is, but planning what will be. So we're not interested in teaching people to manage hospitals, but to develop leaders who can integrate and apply to healthcare the best concepts, such as total quality management and computerized models of thinking, from all kinds of organizations and industries. It's an exciting and unique vision.

"Teamwork and networking are central to The Healthcare Forum's method of leadership development, and we'll continue to stress them. We are encouraging people to attend our conferences as teams rather than just as individuals. Currently, some 40 percent of conference participants are attending as part of a team, which indicates how prevalent is the need for team development.

"In the old days, the state hospital association was the ultimate network. Today healthcare is increasingly a global enterprise. The Healthcare Forum will continue to help groups of like-minded people develop ideas by fostering national and international networking opportunities.

"For example, we have three quality improvement networks as well as a network for COOs, one for emerging leaders, and another on systems thinking. As for international participation, 12 countries are represented at The Forum's 1991 Annual Meeting."

Tough Climb for Women

"It is going to continue to be a very tough climb for women who strive to reach the top. As organizations streamline, fewer positions will be available, and women may not have the opportunity to season themselves and grow. On the positive side, the management ranks are filled with young women coming up. Eventually they will come into their own. I want to be able to look back someday and picture in my mind the people in leadership positions who have succeeded because of my guidance. If I see their name in lights, then I will have been successful."

Discussion Questions

1. Do you agree that "security and maturity" are central to leading a healthcare organization? Why or why not?
2. Do women CEOs reveal a different full range of leadership profile than do men? In what ways?
3. What type of culture do you think this leader creates in her organization? How would you describe it using a visual metaphor?
4. How can such leaders transform cultures?

15

Leadership of Renewal:
Leadership for the 21st Century*

Motorola Incorporated's excellence lies in a deeply bred ability to continually move out along the curve of innovation and to invent new, related applications of technology as fast as older ones become everyday, commodity-type products. In short, it is successful because it is succeeding in renewing itself. Motorola, which commands almost a 50% share of the worldwide market, continues to attract new customers as it makes phones smaller, lighter, cheaper, and easier to use. The company did not achieve its success by accident. Since its inception, Motorola has been managing on the concept of renewal—willing to renew its technologies, and eager to renew the processes by which the institution is run. To ensure that it does not become a victim of its own success, Motorola is stressing, among other things, three key principles: leadership of renewal, renewal of leadership, and thinking the unthinkable.

Motorola's Performance

In the marketplace, Motorola rode the crest of an airwave with seemingly endless reach. More than 50 years after the company invented the HandieTalkie for American soldiers to lug through the battlefields of Europe, portable, wireless, two-way communication is becoming a medium for the masses. Motorola is the preeminent supplier of equipment to a global industry with over 100 million current users.

Motorola, which commands almost a 50 percent share of the worldwide market, continues to attract new customers as it makes phones smaller,

---

*Winston, M. G. (1997). Leadership of renewal: Leadership for the 21st century. *Business Forum, 22*(1), 4–7. (Adapted)

lighter, cheaper, and easier to use. Some cellular operating companies are giving away Motorola's popular MicroTAC phone, which sold for $2,500 just [a decade] ago, to customers who agree to buy cellular service for a certain number of months.

Increasingly multinational, Motorola—which generates more than 60 percent of its revenues overseas—is spreading the wonders of wireless communication to Asia, Eastern Europe, and Latin America. Countries with archaic, state-run phone systems have seized on wireless networks as a relatively inexpensive means of quick stepping into the future. With almost nine billion dollars in semiconductor sales, Motorola has become the world's number three producer of chips, behind Intel and NEC. With the PowerPC, an advanced microprocessor that Motorola developed jointly with IBM and Apple, the company has launched its first serious challenge to Intel's dominance of the all-important market for personal computer chips.

Since 1990, sales have skyrocketed. The company's revenues rose from $10.9 billion in 1990 to $13.3 billion in 1992, $17 billion in 1993, and $22.2 billion in 1994. Sales in 1995 increased 22 percent, to $27 billion, over the previous year, and rose again in 1996 to $28 billion. The increases have been broad-based throughout the company's major businesses, and growth has been highest in international markets. Motorola continues to invest in technology platforms that promise to improve the way people live and work. Key components of this investment included research and development as well as plants and equipment. Special targets were semiconductor, telecommunications, and other electronic products and facilities throughout the world.

Big and sprawling, empowered and reengineered, trained and "TQMed," Motorola now faces a whole new set of challenges—most of them brought on by its own explosive growth. As the company, which has long been dominated by engineers, makes its products more affordable to ordinary consumers not just on-the-move executives, it must become more adept at marketing. As it ventures into more countries—three-quarters of its sales are expected to come from abroad by the end of the decade—it must tailor its approaches to cultures unfamiliar—and perhaps uncomfortable—with concepts like empowerment, decentralization, and cycle time. Above all, **Motorola must work to keep its workers energized, motivated, and dissatisfied—even in the face of the company's much-respected success.**

Motorola's Institutional Heritage

The company did not achieve its success by accident. Since its inception, Motorola has been managing on the concept of renewal, willing to renew its technologies, and eager to renew the processes by which the institution is run. Founded by Paul Galvin 75 years ago, Motorola was built on a bedrock of solid, uncompromising principles. It has always been a company with a distinctive people-oriented culture that incorporates an obsession with quality, uncompromising ethics, and respect for its employees. The foundation of these values was laid by Paul Galvin, a man of limitless intellectual, creative, and conceptual energy. The torch was passed to his son Bob, who ran the company from 1959 until 1990 and masterminded one of the most sweeping corporate transformations in modern times—fighting back against powerful Japanese rivals and remaking Motorola into a world-class competitor in three of the fastest growing electronics markets: cellular telephones, two-way radios, and paging devices.

Responsibility for preserving the institutional heritage now falls primarily upon Gary Tooker, Chairman of the Board; Bob Galvin's son, Chris, Chief Executive Officer; and Bob Growney, President and Chief Operating Officer.

Under Paul Galvin, Motorola pioneered some fairly "radical" employee practices. In 1947, the company started a profit-sharing fund into which the company placed 20 percent of its pretax earnings. In the 1950s, Motorola jettisoned its last punch clock and put all workers on an honor system. Concurrently, the firm created an employee advisory committee that reported directly to the board of directors and separate employee task forces to review such subjects as benefits to ensure that workers got what they needed, not just what managers wanted to give them. Many attribute Motorola's strength to the fact that it is based upon a clear set of principles, not populist programs, because programs have a beginning, a middle, an end, and a "this-too-shall pass" mentality. In contrast, principles are enduring. They are everlasting.

Open to new ideas, devoted to nurturing, and encouraging those who question the oldest assumptions and propose the boldest changes—these are enduring characteristics of Motorola. Several years ago, the Board of Editors of *New Management Magazine* commented, "In no large company of which we are aware has this trait been institutionalized to the extent that it has at Motorola." Motorola has long been characterized as valuing the principles of purposeful motion and proactive anticipation.

To ensure that it does not become a victim of its own success, Motorola is stressing, among other things, three key principles: *Leadership of Renewal, Renewal of Leadership*, and *Thinking the Unthinkable*.

Leadership of Renewal

The global business community is in the midst of a revolution that is shaping how people and organizations will operate and work well into the next century. First, there is the frantic pace of change itself—in technology, geopolitics, and markets—that has left many seemingly invulnerable organizations dazed and perplexed in its wake. Second, computerized information systems have not fully delivered on their promise of lower costs and higher productivity despite three decades of expensive trying. Third, as the problems of industrial Goliaths illustrate, sheer size is no longer enough to ensure domination in a world of faster-moving, more flexible Davids. Fourth, customers and consumers are smarter and more demanding.

In the economy that is emerging, traditional ways of competing have reached a level of parity in which businesses can no longer easily distinguish themselves solely on the basis of quality, technology, product, or price. **An organization's ability to conceptualize and manage change—to compete from the inside out by increasing its capacity for change—has become a competitive advantage in itself.**

To ensure their survival, organizations must create an architecture and support structure conducive to continuous renewal. This task requires that organizations learn to juggle two, apparently contradictory, management priorities simultaneously: maximizing their core businesses and constantly reinventing the company through the infusion of new products, technologies, and people. The continuous-renewal model requires that successful organizations must have in place both an active process for continuous improvement and an energetic plan to identify and carry out breakthrough renewal.

Motorola encourages ongoing reinvention of the company by delivering a consistent message about the need to change; a high-intensity, consistent focus on markets, customers, and competition; consistent benchmarking; and encouraging and rewarding the creation of new industries, not simply new products. Motorola develops a new technology platform at least once every ten years. The company seeks to render its own technologies obsolete before the competition does. Anticipation of change is a religion at Motorola. "Technology roadmaps" assess where breakthroughs are likely to occur, when they can be incorporated into new products, how much money their development will cost, and how the competition is doing.

When the company grasps "straws in the wind" or "gems in the junkpile," it does not hesitate to fund them even before the traditional market studies are completed. The company's Iridium project of 66 low-orbiting satellites (at a projected cost of approximately $4 billion) is a notable example as well as potential problem since this project has run into serious financial difficulties. Decades ago, Motorola committed millions to an emerging technology that many dismissed as a gimmick. That technology is now known as the cellular telephone.

Further, there is the concept of legacy. **All officers must declare a "legacy-leaving" bold goal by which they want their entire career measured.** They will be measured on their attainment of this goal. Also, to ensure that seemingly intractable problems are tackled with a fresh perspective, Motorola has a number of critical processes to encourage the rotation of managers—even the most senior—across business borders. Not only does this lubricate the change process in the business, it refreshes and energizes the executives as well.

The new advertising tag line, "Motorola . . . what you never thought possible™," was coined to underscore the importance of the concept of Leadership of Renewal.

Renewal of Leadership

The new role of leadership is to establish and sustain the organization's proactive, innovative culture. This task requires leaders who can develop an atmosphere of trust and mutual support with their followers so they can identify potential problems before they become crises. Reciprocal loyalty and mutual respect are the hallmarks of the leadership climate created by leaders in this new age. The focus is on achieving high standards of excellence by identifying new potential, seeking out new avenues of opportunity, and activating the human spirit.

The kind of leaders Motorola seeks to develop must find and nurture champions, dramatize goals and direction, build skills and teams, and spread irresistible enthusiasm. They encourage, excite, teach, listen, and facilitate. Their actions are consistent. They pay close attention to their environment, communicate unshakable core values, and patiently develop the skills that enable them to make sustained contributions to their organizations. The focus of development is on continuous self-renewal.

"Management," with its attendant images—cop, referee, devil's advocate, naysayer—connotes controlling. "Leadership" reflects unleashing energy, freeing, building, and supporting. Leaders lead through their ability and willingness to empower their followers, to push power down into the hands of the people so that they have the energy and freedom to seek adventure, creativity, and innovation. Most important, they lead by virtue of caring deeply for their followers, which produces a mutual bond of strong emotional commitment and reciprocal loyalty that are the wellsprings of spirited performance.

Leaders establish the vision and communicate it in a way that helps people link their day-to-day work with the organization's strategic objectives. Leaders shape values. They are supporters, resource providers, obstacle removers, facilitators, consultants, and team builders.

Leaders don't command, control, direct, wield clubs, or shout orders. They generate commitment, not compliance. They enable, empower, trust, and respect—and then get out of the way and let people get results.

Leaders are custodians of the organization's systems. They know that waste, defects, and customer complaints are caused by system defects or unmotivated employees.

Motorola's "Renewal of Leadership" thrust stresses the importance of this kind of leadership with a heart for people and a head for business. The company focuses on performance planning and enhancement (forward-looking) rather than performance appraisal (backward-looking). Tens of thousands of associates are involved in 360-degree feedback initiatives in which individuals get feedback about strengths and development needs from peers, subordinates, managers, and customers. This four-directional feedback process occurs in all regions of the world. An integrated performance leadership system has been introduced to ensure that people are rewarded not only for what they achieve, but also for how. Managers who build up the numbers while tearing down their people are not tolerated. Advancement through the ranks is tied to achieving business objectives through effective deployment and development of people.

Thinking the Unthinkable

Counter-intuitive thinking—the thoughtful process of standing against the crowd and challenging conventional wisdom—is prized, encouraged, and rewarded. In fact, it is the basis on which Motorola's success is founded.

Paul Galvin, the company's founder, failed in his first two businesses because he chose to do what everyone else was doing. He followed the conventional wisdom. Then, he came to discover what would be the essence of Motorola—he discovered the idea of doing the unconventional. He discovered that, paradoxically, by taking risks, by going where others would not go, his firm gained security. Take, for instance, the conventional wisdom when radio was defined as the "home set." Mr. Galvin decided to put it into a car. Everyone told him he was wrong and was making a big mistake. They warned that he was going to lose his company. They asked, "How could anyone possibly drive a car with a radio in it, listen to the news, and concentrate on driving? It will be unsafe. How can they tune in a station, shift with one hand, drive with the other, and push the pedals—simultaneously?"

In 1936, the presidents of Zenith and RCA told Paul that if they had realized the implications of what he was doing, they would have crushed him. Paul discovered the niche that allowed Motorola to survive—focusing on ideas and projects that others wouldn't undertake.

Another Example

On a trip to Europe, Paul realized that there was going to be a war, and, without a Pentagon contract, he developed the two-way radio. He continued to take the unconventional path. Motorola joined the semiconductor business nine months after the transistor was invented. Again, the same critics of the industry—all the conventional wisdom—asked him why he was toying with these things called components. After all, he was in the enter-tainment products, consumer electronics, defense, and automotive busi-ness. They warned him that he was wasting his money.

Early on, Paul's demonstrated behavior and his instinct to be bold proved him right. Over the years, his son Bob had the opportunity to watch and learn from his father. He began to practice these underlying elements: seek the new technology platforms, think in an unconventional way, take risks, act boldly and timely on the anticipation, and always maintain a high value for your employees. We practiced this philosophy, and we gained confidence as we progressed.

As cellular technology was pioneered and refined in the 1960s and early '70s, the pundits doubted that people would pay four-to-six times the cost of their monthly telephone bill to make a call from their purse or car. Again, Motorola ignored conventional wisdom and committed to this technology. Motorola encourages, measures, and rewards each associate, from officer level down to production workers and maintenance people, for challenging conventional wisdom and pushing in new directions. The company makes a cult of dissent and open verbal combat. All employees are entitled—make that expected—to file a "minority report" if they believe their "against-the-grain" views are not being supported. Engineers say they are encouraged to dispute their superiors and one another vigorously at meetings to go for the "breakthrough item."

What of the Future?

Sales in 1996 rose 3 percent to $28 billion from $27 billion in 1995. Earnings were $1.15 billion, compared with $1.78 billion a year earlier. Fully-diluted earnings per common and common equivalent share were $1.90, compared with $2.93 in 1995. Net margin on sales was 4.1 percent for 1996, compared to 6.6 percent in the previous year. Clearly, the company's performance fell short of expectations, but there is every reason for optimism.

Motorola is continuing to invest in programs that create platforms for fu-ture growth without ignoring substantial investments in its core technology businesses. As the year progresses, Motorola expects to reap more of the rewards from its investments in newer digital technologies derived from our core two-way radio, cellular telephones, paging, satellite, and wireless communications businesses. Motorola will continue to create products and technologies that will enable people to improve the way they live and work in ways they never expected.

There is little doubt that Motorola will weather the storm. In today's business environment, where change is necessary for survival, organiza-tions must be willing, able, and eager to change. Motorola is! Success de-pends on adaptability, flexibility, and speed. The ability to move decisively in and out of markets, change product features quickly, and add new value overnight are table stakes in today's global marketplace—the price of simply entering the game. Staying ahead of the rapidly rising change curve requires constant, unrelenting change.

The initiatives that drive quality, cycle time, vision, product development, and excellence in management will continue to ensure Motorola's position as a world leader in the telecommunications arena.

Motorola—a leader in the renewal of renewal.

Discussion Questions

1. How different is Motorola's philosophy of management as compared to your own organization or an organization you know about? In what ways does it differ?

2. What are some potential drawbacks to building a "challenging" culture in your organization?

3. What are some other styles of leadership that could augment the styles already displayed at Motorola?

4. Can a large, old company like Motorola continue to compete in the world of dot.com, high-velocity companies? Is the sharp decline of the price of Motorola stock in 2001 temporary or a sign of things to come?

16

Profiles of Two Successful Women Managers*

Given the record number of women entering the U.S. work force, successful compa-nies will be those that aggressively hire, train, and promote women, and allow these women to express their personal feminine values instead of encouraging women to suppress them. Among those women profiled as successful managers are Barbara Grogan, founder and president of Western Industrial Contractors, and Nancy Badore, executive director of the Ford Motor Company's Executive Development Centre. These women have been very successful at their positions, as the case discusses.

Barbara Grogan, 43, is founder and president of Western Industrial Contrac-tors, a $6 million millwriting firm in Denver Colorado. She started the com-pany with $50,000 and an old pick-up truck in 1972. At the time, construction companies were losing their business base, and many have not survived to this day. But Grogan, one of less than a dozen women among the nearly 5,000 millwrighting contractors nationwide, has not only survived, but has flourished, attracting such clients as AT&T, United Airlines, and IBM.

In 1986, Grogan added a consulting division to provide clients with esti-mating, scheduling, and cost-control services in all phases of the construc-tion business. The consulting company won a $1 million contract to do the scheduling for Denver's new international airport.

Millwrighting involves the moving and installation of industrial equip-ment. Grogan's company has installed the world's largest underground bag-

---

*Tropila, D., & Kleiner, B. H. (1994). Profiles of successful women managers. *Equal Opportu-nities International, 13*(12), 1–6. (Adapted)

gage sorting system at United's O'Hare terminal, hung a four-story theatre screen and relocated $7 million flight simulators used to train airline pilots.

Nancy Badore is the executive director of the Ford Motor Company's Executive Development Centre, which is responsible for training the company's top two thousand managers worldwide in the "new culture" values based on quality and customer orientation. It is this new culture that is credited with enabling Ford to emerge from its near collapse in the early eighties.

Nearly forty-three, Badore joined the company in 1979 as a member of the corporate employee relations staff, where she worked on establishing Ford's Employee Involvement programme, an approach which focused on getting union stewards and plant managers talking with one another.

Soon after, Badore took charge of a project to bring division heads together with plant managers so that division managers could listen to and learn from them. The programme worked so well that her next assignment was to develop a model for permanent structure within Ford that would train the company's executive managers in the programme and keep training them on a continuing basis.

Badore now reports to an executive vice president just below the chairman. Her Executive Development Centre, with its $5 million budget, educates the very top layer of managers and plays a pivotal role in defining the company's direction of change.

Badore is strict about her hours. She comes into the office at 8:30 A.M. and makes sure she is out of the office by 6:00 P.M., so that she and her husband can enjoy quality time with her children. Grogan never goes to the office on weekends and discourages her employees from doing so. They all are willing to put off work-related tasks that did not demand immediate attention in order to prevent business responsibilities from infringing on family time. In fact, general family happiness and fulfillment (contentment) was noted as a way of providing balance and perspective to life, thereby fostering or permitting greater effort and productivity at work.

Discussion Questions

1. Who would you prefer to work for, Barbara Grogan or Nancy Badore? Why?
2. What do you think about Badore's restricting her own hours at the office and encouraging everyone else to do the same?

17

Nimrod Press*

According to Walter Tower, president and CEO of Nimrod Press, entrepreneurs have an immortality complex, and succession planning is not an issue they want to deal with. As Walter grew older, he reluctantly made the decision to turn the position of president and CEO over to his son, Seth. An ongoing conflict ensued as a result, when Walter would act as if he were still in charge by ordering employees around and making changes in the business. He often barked out orders and expected them to be followed. Seth's style of management was more similar to that of a coach than of a boss. His goal was to "see to it that we get all of the collective knowledge of the organization harnessed toward achieving the corporate mission."

NIMROD PRESS

"Entrepreneurs have an immortality complex, and succession is not an issue we want to deal with. This is not an ego trip, but every entrepreneur has to have total confidence in his or her own ideas and abilities at all times."

—Walter Tower

Company Background

Walter Tower, President and CEO, acquired Nimrod Press, a full-service commercial printing company, in the mid-seventies through a leveraged buyout arrangement. Tower, whose experience at that time had been solely

*Wolf, W., Churchill, N. C., & Tower, W. (1994). Nimrod Press (A); Nimrod Press (B). *Entrepreneurship: Theory & Practice, 19*(1), 85–98. (Adapted)

in sales, was confronted with a number of financial and managerial issues during the early years of his leadership.

Walter's View: "Entrepreneurs do not think of buying a company as taking a risk. If we lose, someone else was wrong. When I bought Nimrod Press, I knew that I was going to sell printing and make a lot of money. I didn't know how exactly, but I knew that the market was there and that I'd go get it."

The company weathered its early hardships and Tower succeeded in building the company from a $3 million operation, when acquired, into a $17 million business that now employs 140 people.

The company's specialty is the high-quality, high-technology segment of the commercial/financial printing field. Over the years the company had positioned itself in this niche by investing heavily in state-of-the-art printing presses, advanced computer-based systems for color separation and image manipulation, and automated typesetting systems. Nimrod also has a small art department and an engraved stationery division. By performing a wide range of printing functions, the company could take responsibility for an entire job for a customer, better control the quality of the work and better control scheduling and service for the customer.

Management Style

Walter Tower's passion had always been printing and selling. As he recalls: "I was always very wrapped up in the business and I relied much more on personal dynamics and charisma than on established procedures in dealing with my employees. Benevolent dictatorship is what some people called it, and sometimes not too benevolent. I was working hard, other people looked like they were working hard, so I could excuse them for their shortcomings."

One of the Board members who have worked closely with Walter described his management style: "He has basically been a hands-on, bull-of-the-woods operator. He is the primary decision-maker and he has the feeling that he can talk to anybody in the plant. I think that is an owner-manager's way of operating and he is good at it."

Succession

Walter had four sons, Seth, Vice President; Ethan, CFO; Caleb, in charge of management information systems; and Joshua, away at school, studying for a PhD in physics.

In 1990, Ethan (Walter's son) left Nimrod, deciding that he was not happy with finance and accounting. He wanted to do computer programming and not have a managerial role. According to Walter, Ethan had been on the verge of being fired two or three times and "would have been if he had not been a Tower." Ethan, described as being "very bright, very black and white, with a structured mathematical mind," had difficulty seeing eye to eye with his father. After leaving Nimrod, he started his own computer consulting business.

Walter, who had had several periods of ill health in the past and also had begun to do more frequent traveling as he neared retirement, delegated to [his son] Seth the responsibilities of signing checks in his absence, the advertising function, and involvement with various senior management groups. With Ethan having left the company and son Caleb having less experience, it was assumed that one day Seth would be asked to run the business; however, it wasn't discussed much. On several occasions when Walter went away for about six weeks, he asked Seth to run the company, as well as the Board meetings, in his absence. Seth began to make some changes, such as setting up management committees and delegating more responsibilities downward within the organization. However, when Walter returned from his trips, his own management style overrode Seth's, causing Seth to become increasingly frustrated.

According to Walter: "I don't think I ever really thought about the time when I would turn over the company; it was the Board of Directors who pointed out that succession was an issue to be thought about. With Ethan's leaving the company and Caleb (another son) just starting with us, Seth was the obvious choice. He had grown in the sales department and in an abstract sense he was it in succession, so that took care of that. I knew he was coming along over the last couple of years, but this business gets kind of frenetic. Seth's office was the closest to mine but I saw him less often than people at the other end of the building. He was busy selling his printing and I was busy running the plant and there was really not a lot of transfer of information going on. What's going to happen with Seth running the company is going to happen, and besides, he's a good, sound young man. He's well educated, he's experienced in the business. He's got good people skills. I'm not worried about it, so why think about the issue? I tried really as often as I thought about it to bring Seth into decisions, but there's only one way to learn to swim. Reading a book does not do it. Practicing on land does not do it. You have to get in the water. Get your hair wet and you'll learn to swim."

According to Seth: "I think that Walter recognized that I was perhaps going through a period of time when I felt like Prince Charles, never knowing when his mother was going to die and he would take over the throne. So he wanted to start the transfer process, and he was looking at his 'second career' as he calls it. So we put together a plan. I brought in a sales assistant who took over a large portion of my day-to-day handling of clients, although it did take a period of a year and a half to two years to get her properly trained and get the credibility with my clients. So that was sort of our transition plan and there were other things that were identified that I would start to phase over to this person and that person. Then, all of a sudden, I felt like I had transitioned myself out of a job because Walter's health was much better and his desire to stay involved in the business had grown more." There was a time when Walter would say, "How quickly can you take over the company?" And then the next day or in the next breath, he'd say, "in 3 to 5 years when you're ready."

Caleb made the decision in 1991 to take a leave of absence from Nimrod to go to graduate school full-time at Northwestern University. He found it difficult to leave but didn't believe that there was anywhere to move within the company since Seth was so obviously heir-apparent.

Just prior to Caleb's departure, Winston Chamberlain, a Director of the Company and Professor of Business Administration, had invited Walter, and then Seth and Caleb, to two separate sessions of his entrepreneurship class to speak about family business. When the students commented that it was hard to believe that Walter and the two younger Towers had been talking about the same business, the generation gap between father and sons became apparent to Professor Chamberlain. So Winston went to Seth and asked informally if he might want to see someone of his own age bracket represented on the Board. Seth agreed wholeheartedly.

Members of the Nimrod management team as well as Tower family members regularly attended the Board of Directors' meetings to make presentations and get a better understanding of the company's operations. For this reason, an Executive session was always held at the end of each Board meeting with only Walter and Board members in attendance. At the Executive session in October of 1991 the issue of succession resurfaced. The discussion began when someone brought up the fact that all of the Board members were 60 and over, and if Seth were going to become president, it would be a good idea to put somebody from his generation on the Board.

The Board members tentatively approved the nomination of Joe Zock, a financial investment advisor in his late 30s and a friend from Seth's college days. Joe was invited to attend the next Board meeting and, near the end of the session, was asked to become a regular member. At that point somebody said to Walter, "Well, now that Joe is here, when are you going to make Seth president?" He replied, "I don't know." So somebody else said, "Well, how about now?" And Walter said, "Well, yes, I guess so."

Walter brought Seth into the meeting and asked if he wanted the job. He said, "Yes, if, in fact, you mean that I'll be chief executive officer. I don't want the title and not be able to do the job." Walter said, "You're president and CEO and the Board has agreed." Seth replied: "If that's the job you're talking about, then I am interested in it and I would like to take the job." So there were congratulations and handshakes and someone said, "Now that you've got it, your biggest problem will be to get rid of the old man."

"After Walter finally offered me (Seth) the job at the October Board meeting and I had accepted it, he said to me, 'Well, think about it over the weekend and we'll talk on Monday.' And he spent the next three days trying to talk me out of it."

—Seth Tower

The Early Transition

Employee: "I think it's always been clear that the transition was going to take place. It was never clear as to when. Seth has always said, 'It's going to be sooner rather than later.' Walter had always said, 'I'll know when it's time and that may be soon and it may not be soon.' When the transition decision was made at the Board meeting, Seth had not been expecting it. Walter had not really expected it. The Board had been pushing for it, and all of a sudden it happened. Not that the timing was too abrupt or that the transition was too fast, it's just that there were certain basic issues that were not worked out ahead of time. Walter and Seth decided to sort of swap roles but they didn't talk about how they were going to have an orderly transition of power and even more importantly they didn't come up with an agenda for what Walter was going to be doing for the rest of his life. Consequently what happened was all of a sudden the decisions were landing on Seth's desk and Walter was to be kept out of the loop in terms of making decisions until Seth brought them to him. There was no job description created for him, and frankly, he wasn't really allowed to do very much. I think that was a tremendous problem."

Employee: "In the beginning, there were clearly times when Seth left the building for lunch and Walter would try and turn the place upside down. Walter has a very entrepreneurial style and if something is not being done that he thinks should be done, he wants it done. And if there's something not going right, he's not the most patient guy around. So for the first 60 or 90 days, if Seth was out of the office for a few days, Walter would just start rattling cages and he'd start changing things."

Walter's Current Role

Walter: "My title is Chairman. However in *The Godfather*, my role would be consigliore. You know, I nose around and I see things and I ask questions. I try not to give anybody answers except about work that I've sold. But I think part of my job is asking questions; asking the right questions. I'm growing better and better at going through Seth rather than saying directly to someone do it this way or do it that way. . . .

"What is important to me is security. I'm too old to go back out and peddle printing and earn a couple of hundred thousand dollars a year. I tried that. The first thing I did after Seth became president was to fill my brief case with samples and go out and make calls. I discovered, I'm not the kid I was 20 years ago and the 20- to 30-year-olds that are buying printing today don't want to see an old fart. And those that are willing to see me want to make their own mistakes. I'm just so used to saying, 'Hey, that's not the way to do it, you do it this way.' Occasionally you can get away with that and there are a dozen or so Nimrod customers who are perfectly willing to go that route and use my experience and use it properly and successfully. And that's great. I'll do a major amount of their business."

CFO: "Walter comes in every day. He comes in most Saturdays. He's ever present and that didn't change. And, in fact, if anything at the beginning, he probably showed up more. But he's always still around."

Seth's Role

Seth: "I always wanted to run a business. That was my ambition when I studied business administration. I thought I would end up working for a big corporation some place and I figured that one of the quickest routes into upper management was through the sales department. But I never saw myself as somebody who would always sell printing and I think that's one of the biggest disappointments Walter's had because he loves to sell printing and I don't. I did a fairly good job selling printing. I like talking to the clients and I have fun along the way, but it is far from being my lifelong ambition. Walter would have been happy just selling printing all his life. When he bought the company, he brought somebody in here to run it so he could sell printing. To me, selling printing was a means to an end. And the end was to get here, behind this desk."

Perspectives on the Transition

Seth: "Walter's still very active. He tends to go around and behave the way he did before when he was running the company. There are times when he calls people in the office and says, 'God damn it, go out and do it this way.' The employee will come to me and say, 'Seth, Walter wants me to do it this way.' And I say, 'No, that's not what we want to do. I'll take care of Walter. You know what we want to do, we've discussed it.' Being the entrepreneurial-spirited person Walter is, he has a habit of telling people what to do and how to do it which works to a certain extent in an entrepreneurial organization. I don't believe in that. I don't think that I can tell people how to do their jobs nor do I want to tell them how to do their jobs. But it is my job to see to it that we get all of the collective knowledge of the organization harnessed toward achieving our corporate missions, our goals, or whatever. I believe I'm more of a coach than I am a dictator so that when I talk with the senior managers, who Walter is the most prone to meddle with, I can sit down and say, 'Look, we know we're working toward this goal. Walter is my problem. I will go see him and deal with this.' And when I go in I'll say, 'Look, Walter, I've got a problem because this is what we are working on and this is what I'm trying to do. If you don't like the way I'm running the company, you can fire me. It's a business decision. If you don't like the way your company is being run, then get rid of me.' But then he'll say, 'Oh no, no, that's not what I want.' Of course, what he wants me to do is to do it the way he would do it. And I can't, that's not the natural thing for me to do. That's not the way I want to conduct business."

Walter: "I don't really think my being around has been Seth's biggest problem. But it's been a major one. And letting go obviously has been a major issue for me. I think if you own a company for 20 years and you get into the habit of running it and people get in the habit of coming to you for answers, those habits are hard to break. It would have been awfully nice if my wife and I could have taken six months off to take a boat trip around the world or whatever, but due to other family commitments that wasn't possible. It would have been a good thing to do to let Seth start out with his own slate without me sitting in the next office but it didn't happen that way."

Seth: "We've been restructuring the organization. Putting the proper talents to work in the proper management positions in the organization. We have one department that was essentially doing the same thing with two management systems, two sets of paperwork, two sets of employees, and it just wasn't working. So there was a restructuring of personnel from that standpoint. When I took over in October 1991, I think we had 164 employees and we've got 138 today. And we are doing more business today than we were then; there was a lot of extraneous stuff."

Additional Reactions to the Transition

Walter: "Seth's and my relationship has always been reasonably collegial. The hard part has been for me to step back and he has forced that issue quite rightly. For example, one day Seth came into my office when I was answering a question for somebody and said, 'What the hell are you doing? I'm supposed to answer that. I wish you'd send them to me. I'm the president of the company.' After a year and quarter, the only real serious area where I'm meddling, if meddling is the right word when I concern myself with minutia, is in the finance area. This is for two reasons. One, I've had more experience in it and, as I said before, my name is on the back of the paper at the bank. Also, all my retirement income is tied up here."

Seth: At some point the bird's gotta fly out of the nest. You can't be there stringing him along. So there have been a lot of times since then when I have had to look at him and say, 'Walter, if you aren't happy with this decision we can change. You can take over the company again. You own the stock. I'll get out of your way. I'm not going to stick around and sell printing. But I'll find something else to do and you can run your company.' But he says, 'Oh no, no, I don't want you to do that.' But there are days when he wants to be involved and he wants to run his company. And it's very difficult because the message that gets sent to the employees is mixed. Well, I have to grab the employees and say, 'Walter's my problem. Walter's not your problem. If he tells you to do something, you do it but you gotta come to me and let me know what you're doing and if I have a problem with it, then I'll take it up with Walter. You don't have to deal with that problem. We've got to focus the attention.' It was very difficult in the beginning because I think at the outset if you had asked nine out of ten employees at Christmas of 1991 who was running the company even though I was supposedly the CEO, they would have said 'Walter.' At Christmas 1992, you might get 60% of them saying that Seth runs the company and 40% would probably still say, 'Well, Walter really runs the company.' . . .

"I think that the relationship with Walter is kind of contrived at this point because there have been times when he's wanted me to seek his advice and I haven't. And there are times when I've sought his advice and he said, well, that's your problem now. So it's contrived in the sense that he would really like to give me advice, but if I ask for it he doesn't want to give it to me and if he gives it to me I don't want to take it. It's very frustrating. He wants me to use him, but he wants to contribute on his terms. I need him to contribute on my terms. The terms are different and we haven't necessarily found a good common ground. I think the farther he gets removed from the business, the easier it will be for him to provide what I want him to provide. I like to be able to get advice from him, a different approach to doing it. It doesn't necessarily mean I'll take it, but I like to get a different perspective. I think that has been a problem too, because when he does give advice, I don't immediately go out and do what he said. 'This is what you do and this how you do it' is the way he gives advice."

Director: "I'd say the transition has gone quite well. Quite well and I think part of that is Walter's being out of the office quite a bit. I would have to give Walter some credit for giving Seth a run. Letting him run. On the other hand once he gets on a hot subject, Walter can be Walter, because nobody knows as much about anything as he does. And he truly does understand the business fully. So if he's into a debate he can be pretty strong."

June (Walter's wife):   "I think on Walter's side. At a very logical level, he probably expected not to have a lot of involvement. But I think on an emotional level he thought he would have more involvement than he has. And with Seth, I think it's probably the reverse. Seth probably, hopefully, thought that he would have more control and his father would go away, be out of the picture more than he has been. And I think in Walter's case he didn't think it through in this way and sort of thought he would still be involved in some way."

CFO: "The transition is far more dramatic than I'd ever imagined it could possibly be. There were a lot of side bets going that Walter was not going to be able to pull out of this thing and he couldn't give up the hands-on, rattle the cage, style of management that he's been used to."

Seth: "The transition will take as long as my father lives. That's just the way he is. He's always going to want to have some say in this organization even if he gives up all his stock. Even if we were to sell the organization, completely sell all the stock and get out, I'm not sure that Walter would agree to it unless he had some sort of consulting role with the new owners so that he could come in and give them his two cents worth about the company he built. That's the way he is. It's going to be difficult."

HR Manager: "Well, I think that it's gone better than I expected. I'm surprised that Walter has turned over the reins so easily. I didn't think it would happen that way. You see I've been with him now for 21 years so I have mixed emotions on this. Walter's style, I've just been used to it so it's a big transition for me. But it has gone smoother than I expected. Walter he's a doer. He sees a problem, he reacts immediately. Seth is completely different. He has to think about it. In certain situations he will have quite a few meetings over an issue. He's more methodical than his father so things don't get done that fast, but maybe they get done better."

Discussion Questions

1. How could Seth and Walter have led the leadership transition at Nimrod Press more effectively?
2. What are some of the problems that Walter is displaying with this transition in terms of his capacity to follow Seth?

3. What impact do you think this leadership transition is having, and will have in the future, on the leadership culture at Nimrod Press?

4. How would you integrate the two leadership orientations of Seth and Walter to maximize the future potential of Nimrod Press?

5. How might you apply what you know about intellectual stimulation to address what you consider to be the central problem in this case?

III

STRATEGIES AND THEIR IMPLEMENTATION

Leaders are ultimately involved in the strategic decisions of consequence to their organization. This section begins with seeing how ineffective leadership can be damaging to a firm. Another issue discussed is how successful leadership is needed for a firm to make "right angle" turns in response to sharp changes in its market and environment. Also, we examine the ways a business leader can be transformational and transactional. The cases in this section are as follows:

18. The Future at Telview
19. David Glassman: Division Manager in Telview
20. Joan Rivers' Memo
21. Back to the Past When the Future Seemed So Obvious
22. Amy's Debrief
23. A Doll's House

18

The Future at Telview*

Jim Cummings, CEO of Telview's new parent company, sent a memo to the employees of Teleview. Cummings expressed to the employees that the market they are in is changing rapidly. The old way of business, which was based on long product development times, is not profitable any longer. Telview has to be smaller, leaner, faster, more agile, and more flexible in bringing solutions to the marketplace. Jim Cummings appears to be attempting to lead employees by explaining what they should do to help achieve company goals rather than what they could do to achieve their own goals.

Recently, the senior management of Telview received copies of the attached memo from their new parent corporation's CEO. One of the senior managers just handed you the material and said, "There is some evidence of leadership out there!" What do you think he meant, and how would you respond to the questions at the end of the case?

Following this memo [in case 19] is an interview with one senior manager at Telview, who commented on events taking place at the organization.

TO: Telview Employees

FROM: Jim Cummings, CEO

In a recent memo to you, I talked about the need for Telview to make what I call "a right-angle turn." I also challenged us to work together to make Telview a recognized leader in mission-critical networks.

---

*An original case written by the editors.

Your response to that memo has been overwhelmingly positive. My sense is that you feel we're heading in the right direction, you're excited about the opportunities, and you're committed to helping us achieve our goals. That's extremely encouraging to me. Extremely!

Of equal importance, our new direction has captured the imagination of the outside world. Industry consultants, the financial community, key opinion leaders, the media and, most importantly, our customers are rallying around our new vision of "webnext." And that's good news. External validation by these key players reinforces that we're on the right path.

Achieving the right-angle turn, however, requires that we focus far beyond just the business implications of webnext. We must also bring about a fundamental culture change within Telview. And that's what I'd like to discuss here.

Let me begin by answering an obvious question: Why do we need to change?

The answer is simple: The market in which we're competing has changed drastically, and so has our competition. In addition to competing against our traditional competitors, we're also going head to head with the best in the computing industry, the best in the consumer electronics industry, and the best in the data networking industry. And these new competitors were born and raised in an environment vastly different from the one we grew up in.

These new competitors come from an unregulated, extremely competitive environment, one dominated by short product development cycles and short times to market. The world of "very short."

Our "traditional" competitors, on the other hand, grew up in a regulated, standards-driven climate characterized by long product development cycles and long times to market. It was the world of "very long."

Very long used to be okay because, for the most part, we were designing and manufacturing very large, very complex, and very expensive network systems, primarily for customers with a market monopoly. Moreover, because these systems represented huge financial bets for us, we had to get it right; the risk to the corporation and our customers was too high to make mistakes. Consequently, our number one priority was to ensure that our designs were absolutely perfect. Because perfection took time, however, we were often very late to market. Being late was not particularly problematic, though, because there was little competition. In the world of very long, the market window was literally open for years. So, we believed that our customers should wait for perfection.

Today's customers, however, even our most loyal ones, cannot afford to wait. The industry is changing so quickly that market windows open and close in real time, and new customers and new suppliers emerge daily. As a result of deregulation and increased competition, our customers have a range of choices like they've never had before. If we can't develop and deliver a solution that will make them competitive in the time frame they require, they will go to a supplier who can.

This pace is exactly why we need to adopt new ways of doing business, ways more attuned to the world of the very short cycle. If we are going to continue to be successful, we need to keep our customers successful; to do that, we need to embrace some of the thinking, behaviors, and processes that are characteristic of our new competitors, competitors who are typically smaller, leaner, and faster than we are; who have fewer bureaucratic processes; and who are typically more agile and flexible in bringing solutions to the marketplace.

Although we're competing in the new world of very short, in many ways our culture is still very much anchored in the world of long, comfortable cycle times. And that's what we need to change quickly.

The fundamental change that I think must take place is this: We must redefine our internal value system. We must stop valuing internal definitions of perfection and start valuing our ability to hit a market window at the right time with an offer that the customer sees as being much better than our competitors'.

And that really is a different way of doing business in Telview. Our history has taught us to incorporate every feature imaginable, to use each new product as an opportunity to pioneer new technology, and to sacrifice time to market to minimize risk. I'm now asking you to learn how to manage risk to ensure all new product developments are on time. Why? Because the greatest risk that we and our customers face today is missing the market window. To miss it, is to lose the opportunity forever.

Let me share with you some of my own thoughts on the culture change that needs to take place.

First and foremost, we need to ensure that we truly have a "Customer First" mindset. All employees, no matter what their function, must understand that Telview's number one priority is helping our customers be successful. Our customers' success, and ultimately our's, depends on our ability to deliver what we say we will achieve within the committed time frame.

Second, let's not presume to know what the customer needs. Rather, let's engage our customers early in the process, work closely with them to fully understand where they place their value, and then put our energy and focus into delivering that customer-defined value.

Let's do everything we can to make our customers competitive TODAY! If we can use existing technology—either our own or sourced externally—to meet a customer's immediate need, let's do so, and then, if appropriate, evolve to a more sophisticated design.

On any new product development, let's ensure we know the answers to two key questions:

1. What are the minimum new capabilities that we must bring to market in order for the customer to choose us over our leading competitor?
2. When must we deliver this product to a leading customer if we hope to win their business and lead the industry?

Let's not always value the technologically elegant solutions that are perhaps months or even years away from being available when another solution, although perhaps not as elegant, can be delivered much more quickly.

Let's really think hard about whether or not there's any value in starting development projects that will not be available for general release within 18 months. . . . If we cannot get the product to market within that time frame, I'd suggest we've probably defined an uncompetitive product.

Let's begin to make smaller bets, and a lot more of them. Rather than continually looking for multiyear mega projects, let's encourage a more entrepreneurial type of hitting those market windows of opportunity. In the world of very short, we can't afford to squander time, or new opportunities.

Some of the thoughts I've shared in this memo will be explored in more depth at the end of this month, at my CEO Forum, a new strategic planning session that will replace what was known in the past as the Senior Management Committee. The theme of this first forum is "Making the Right-Angle Turn." I'm looking forward to sharing the outcome with you in a future correspondence.

In summary, I encourage you to challenge our traditional ways of working, thinking, and behaving so we can make the changes necessary to survive and succeed in the world of very short.

Yours sincerely,
Jim Cummings

P.S. To respond to this letter, please send your e-mail to "CEO's Office."

Discussion Questions

Consider that everyone in your team received the same e-mail from Jim Cummings, and you've decided to discuss it with your team before sending him a reply.

1. Does Cummings inspire your team and you with his e-mail letter? If yes, why? If no, why not?
2. To respond to Cummings, what might you do to *intellectually stimulate* your team and yourself to come up with feasible and innovative answers?

3. What kinds of assumptions won't get you very far? What kinds of assumptions will?
4. Can you think of metaphors for culture change and for competitive products?
5. How do you have to work with your employees now to develop their full potential?

19

David Glassman:
Division Manager in Telview*

David Glassman is a division manager at Telview. The company has lately fallen into a decline. It is a technology-based organization. The company has to change its business strategy to survive in the future. It has to deal with a global market rather then a local market.

David places an emphasis on social interactions within his division. He feels that his people are the best. He promotes into management positions employees who have both technological and people skills. David relies on his managers to deal with operations and management of employees. He does not like to undermine the ability of his managers to do their jobs. He thinks that people in the division feel that those who work hard are promoted. Following is an interview with David.

Q: Describe the situation in your organization and its implications for your division.

A: The situation here has been so strong in the past few years, but there were changes in the market that affected us. We are still profitable, but the profits are not very big. We hope that it is not a sign of the future, but it requires our attention. It's not a good situation, but so far we have not cut into the flesh, we have less coffee and maybe less overtime, but people's ears certainly are tuned into what is being said. However, the people in technologies (which, in our perception,

---

*An original case written by the editors.

we are a part of) believe that our company should accelerate the change process. Currently, there is no atmosphere of crisis, but we have to improve and develop in the technologies area.

These people know that they can work outside our company, and these people are not attached to the company. When they begin to leave in large numbers, we will know that we are in a crisis.

Q: How do you present the situation to your employees?

A: I explain it as a period where we are in decline, so we can be even further up in the future. We organize ourselves differently. We used to trust the local market, but now we have to work globally and this is a challenge in which we have to reorganize the structure. I don't see the black clouds. I say it because I believe in what we can do.

Q: What are your organization's goals, and what are the goals of your division?

A: The goals of our company divide between employees and owners. The owners want to make money and quickly, especially the new owners. I don't think that it is immoral on their behalf, but it may have implications. I have been working here for years and there has always been a feeling of home here. I believe that is still the situation; it has not changed as yet. We always had the goal of taking care of people. We began in our region as the main source of employment. We have received waves of immigration (including myself from 1973). We hired new immigrants when nobody trusted them. This is a workplace beyond the need to make money. I also want to make money, but this special atmosphere is very important to me, and people say that here more than other places there is a feeling of home. Maybe the young people are less attached, but even they say so as well. We teach each other and we don't hide from each other, unlike other high-tech cultures where people hide their knowledge from each other to maintain their advantage. Here we share. This is more than a working place—this is a home.

Q: Can the new owners' goals hurt this culture?

A: I think that people will understand the need to cut costs. After all, it happens in families too. The young people—the high tech—are less attached to where they work, they care for their self-development, and they may move because they are more prone to that. But most people will be cooperative if they will understand where we are going.

Q: I interviewed people from different divisions who did not mention social goals as you did. Do you think this is unique to your division?

A: I don't want to be seen as arrogant, but there is a special atmosphere in this division. That's what people from other parts of the organization say to me. Maybe in other divisions, they put less emphasis on working together, but here it is very important to us. People here also need new computers, but they realize the importance of social ties.

Q: Do you have any opposition from top management with regard to your policies?

A: I did not see any opposition. We never required more money than other divisions for our activities; we manage with the same money that others get. Moreover, we pay our engineers less than what they get in technologies. They make more over there due to the structure of the market. They are not better, although my people make less and they know it. We have to work with other methods. When they cut for others, they also cut for us.

Q: How do you disseminate your policies down the organizational hierarchy to department and team managers, and to employees?

A: I did not come from outside. I did not have to change. I appointed people who understand the importance of social relationships. I will not appoint others. Yes, they have technical skills, but they must have social skills, too. Similarly, team managers are chosen in an extremely slow process compared to other divisions. We examine whether they have social skills before we appoint them. Because many people have technical skills and not social skills we created a position: "technological leader." This position is for people who need to be promoted but cannot be managers. Therefore, I do not really have to disseminate the information—it is inherent in our activities. The managers know that this is part of their job. We have some meetings where we emphasize it, but this is minor.

Individualized Consideration

Q: How do you learn about your employees' specific needs?

A: I cannot manage everybody. I manage my managers who manage their employees. I make sure, however, that I have meetings with my direct followers once a week. I don't cancel these meetings for other things. We also instituted a system of feedback meetings, and I learn from these. In part of the meeting with managers we discuss HR [human resources] issues, we also talk about people specifically, and we talk about what we find from the feedback process. We talk about the relationships with me, too. It is convenient that we can all talk like that.

Q: Do you learn about specific individuals during those meetings?

A: Yes. I ask. I am especially interested in the team managers and the people who are leading in their departments. I make sure that I know if they are bored or not. I am personally interested in those with managerial potential or technical potential. About the others, I am interested in the weak or in difficulties that people have. I am especially interested in the way new people are absorbed into departments. But I let my department managers take care of the rest of the people. I allow myself to be less involved because the department managers are very good at doing this.

Q: Do your managers [that are under you] conduct similar meetings?

A: Yes, they do, or I hope they do. Some of them do it more, some less.

Q: Are there interactions with people in the corridor? Can you describe it?

A: There are a lot of interactions. I am a very optimistic person and tend to be in a good mood even when there is trouble. I know, however, how to sense people's moods. For example, when I ask how is a person doing and the "yes" he or she gives me is not convincing, I ask for more information. I don't deal with problems in the corridor, but I ask the person to fix a meeting with me. It is not nice to arrange meetings in the corridor. It is fun to go around and ask questions. I am from this division, and I love communication with people—these are my friends, I like to joke with them sometimes.

Q: If somebody approaches you directly about a problem, how do you deal with it?

A: First of all, I allow everybody to come. I am not angry with people who do so. I begin with stressing that it is important that a department manager know about the problem. However, if the employee prefers that the information not pass to his or her manager, I respect that position. For example, I had a person who wanted to move to another part of the company, so first of all I asked him if he spoke with the department head. We can not hide it from her, after all! However, I encourage people to move within the organization. I asked him to talk to the department manager as soon as she returned from her vacation. The treatment of these problems should be in the hands of department managers, but I listen to people's problems.

Inspirational Motivation

Q: What do you do that makes your employees work harder?

A: I think that people here feel that the work *contributes to them*. This is very important. It is important that they deal with high-level technology. This is easy, because communication is a leading technology. They have to understand that they are advancing personally because of their work. The best will be promoted, the best will become managers. I was interviewed by the company newspaper regarding whether I am disturbed by the fact that manager(s) in other department(s) and divisions grew in my division. It is not easy to train people to be good enough to leave you. But this is how you keep the best here (knocking on the table). It is a paradox. You teach people to be good, then they leave, but they know that they have a future. I tell people that it is worthwhile to work here, they will learn, they will get tools, they will learn how to work with customers—they will learn and learn, and that is what's pushing them.

Q: How do you present work issues? Do you use enthusiasm?

A: The truth is that the domain we are in makes me very enthusiastic. It is like nurturing a special unit in the military, like the parachutists. We want to give people the feeling that they are the best, and also train them to be the best. It is hard but we know how to do it.

Q: How do you see your division in 5 years, and how do you express it to the employees?

A: We have a goal to be the central body in developing the quality of products. Maybe it is pretentious, but it is important. Some argue that testing of products should be part of R&D or technologies, but we are successful and that's why we develop. People wanted to break it down. My main goal is that we will continue and move on to other new issues. We are more than a checkup unit—we move into adjacent areas and if the company goes into new markets we should be ready to support it.

Passive Leadership

Q: Was there a situation in which your employees thought you were passive, and it was hard to get hold of you?

A: Since I took on the job of selling to the former Soviet republics, I am gone sometimes. However, I feel that the division has the best managers, and they have all the authority they need, so they can make their own decisions. I don't cancel meetings with people, but I am less involved with employees personally. I don't think I should be involved even if I am here. This is why I have department managers, who also have team managers. However, I keep in touch with my managers regularly.

Intellectual Stimulation

Q: How do you view your employees' thinking style, especially in terms of the diversity among them?

A: There are some procedures, but not too many, in my opinion. These procedures should help us get where we need to get. We use procedures only when we have to. We are not so formal, and it encourages people to think. When we had a lack of personnel, people complained that they did not have time to come up with new ideas, but in general we are open. I prefer that people argue and have more ideas, although I talk confidently and I have confidence in myself. I grew up here and it makes me a bad manager in this sense because I know a lot about the work we do and am very confident in myself. I realize that it may limit other people's ideas. However, if people have different ideas, I listen.

Q: What do you do if a team or any employee is stuck on a project?

A: I do not like to "land" [to come from above] on people. With time, I do it even less. When I approach, it does not add much value if I approach the people. I work with team managers and department managers. I don't ask people what they did or they did not do. I don't take over meetings. This is the responsibility of the managers below me. For example, in the "Even Split" project, the team was in trouble, the developers screwed it up, and during the testing period my people had to pay for their mistakes. In the meeting, we had emphasized that it is not their fault, there was an error and it had to be corrected, which implied more work for them. My job was to encourage them to solve the problem, not necessarily to solve the problem for them. They have their immediate managers who can give them the technical assistance they need. With regard to the technical parts, I discuss it with the managers, with whom there is no risk of me landing from above. The managers can see the legitimacy of my intervention, and it is value adding.

Constructive Transactional-Contingent Reward

Q: Do people who work harder in the division indeed get more than others? Is there an atmosphere of one to one (quid pro quo)?

A: I think that people who work harder get more. This is why all the managers who were here grew here. They received more because they worked harder. With regard to bonuses it is more difficult, but I try to keep the link between bonus and input. I make sure that the bad employees do not get bonuses. I would like to believe that the people who work here perform well, and that they know that it pays off to work well. But there may be some differences among departments and I am not much aware about what new people think about what they get in return for their effort.

Q: How are goals determined in the division?

A: This is a different division. Our departments work independent of each other. Each department works on a different platform. They don't communicate with each other. Our meetings do not focus on what happens in each platform because it is not interesting. Our meetings focus on how we can improve our work, how we take care of people.

Q: How do you define goals, trace performance, and encourage fulfilling the goals?

A: In the division meetings that we hold once every half a year, I focus on giving them my message or vision, not on reporting. I emphasize our vision, that we need to absorb new people, and we create an open meeting where we ask about people's problems. I prefer to write down what they say instead of giving them a verbal response. If there is a need we arrange meetings to discuss specific things.

Management by Exception

Q: How do you ensure that people in the division do not make mistakes?

A: We have two ways. First, it is essential to learn from mistakes. We are doing causal analysis. The process is not directed toward the past, but instead on what we can do differently to be better in the future. I don't necessarily participate, because I believe the atmosphere can be better if a top manager is absent, so people will not be afraid to talk about their mistakes and learn from them.

Q: How much of your time do you spend dealing with mistakes?

A: I don't invest much time in mistakes. I mainly try to see what we can do better in the future, even if the mistake was severe. I focus on whether we learned from the mistake and how we can prevent it in the future.

Q: Does top management approach you with mistakes in a harsh way? How do you approach those under you?

A: We should be able to explain our mistakes, this is part of the conditions we get from the company. There is no landing from above [vice president or CEO] on our people directly—it goes through me.

Q: Repeating the same question.

A: There are people above who are too busy with mistakes. These people do not approach people from the division directly, although they approach me. When they approach me, I bridge between them and top management. However, I do transfer the information.

Q: How can you bridge such messages?

A: I do not transfer different information. There has never been a situation that I learned about something inside from top management. Whenever I was asked about a mistake we made, I already knew about it. I am the first one to know. Either I have an answer or I get back to them after I check it. I ask department managers to investigate and explain their findings. We never change the explanations we get.

Q: Influence tactics: How do you convince your employees to agree with you?

A: I use emotion. "It is what we need to do," or "It is important." I focus a
lot on explaining what to do and the goals and what not to do.

Humor

David noted: "I use humor a lot in my work, and also at home. I use it a lot
to relieve tension. I learned from experience and workshops that it is helpful. I don't like long and difficult discussions. Humor makes people feel
better, they enjoy it, and I think it adds to the atmosphere and makes others feel better, too. It think that we have a healthy atmosphere and openness. People come and tell me a joke."

Discussion Questions

1. What did you like most about David's style of leadership? What did you
   like least?
2. How do you think his division will do during the transformation process at Telview? Why?
3. What type of feedback would you give David to enhance his leadership
   style?
4. What aspects of David's style do you feel you could adopt and develop
   in your own style of leadership?
5. What was David's most important message?

20

Joan Rivers' Memo*

Joan Rivers, CEO, sent a memo to the employees of NBx. Her message was that she would like to reengineer the fundamental business processes of the organization. The NBx line of business is the research and development (R&D) of new products. The processes by which the organization reviews and undertakes projects is outdated and prevents many of the projects from meeting the windows of opportunity they need to be profitable.

Joan suggested that the organization should focus on the needs of individual projects rather then trying to use a one-size-fits-all approach to managing all R&D projects. She would like to see a focus on company objectives and a collective effort to make NBx the most valued company in the industry.

To: NBx Employees

From: CEO Joan Rivers

Subject: GAP Reviews

GAP Reviews

In 1985, when I was president of ABC, I introduced the step review process. It was developed at a time when our new technology releases had doubled in size, and we were struggling to regain control of the quality and schedules of the software loads that we were shipping to our large installed base.

---

*An original case written by the editors.

The concept behind the original process was quite simple, and was aimed at doing a better job of managing the risks associated with bringing our new products to market. The initial process had only four steps. *Step zero* was to launch a new business opportunity. *Step one* was intended to launch a serious product development program and project team. *Step two* meant we were ready for field trial. *Step three* indicated that we were ready for full commercial release.

The heads of the strategic business units (SBUs) were to hold the reviews with their design teams. The goal was to ensure that (a) the team put all the facts on the table regarding the risks it faced in entering the next phase of commercialization, and (b) the team had appropriate plans and contingencies in place to deal with these risks as it moved forward. The process has evolved over the years, with attendance becoming larger, more steps being added, and, more often than not, the reviews no longer being chaired by the general manager (GM) of the SBU.

I am convinced that today, as currently practiced, the step review process is slowing us down. I must admit that it is simply outdated. If I were to assume that we allowed just 3 months between reviews, then we now have a process that would require 21 months to complete. This is just too slow! I also feel the reviews are not being used with a determination to hit our schedule, but rather as an opportunity to redefine the schedule and consequently miss our market commitments.

When we introduced the step review process, it governed when we would ship the next technology release to our installed base. As we move into competing for the right to build new software products, we are finding ourselves up against very fast competitors who typically have a very simple development process (i.e., Alpha, Beta, Ship). Their process has the sole purpose of focusing on the market window, and getting to market ASAP!

Funding

In February of 1998 we reengineered our business time limits and incorporated many improvements in teamwork and speed of decision making. For any new product development cycle, the real focus of the discussion must now be on the following:

- What are the total capabilities that we must bring to market to have the customer choose us over our leading competitor?
- When must we deliver this product to a leading customer if we hope to win their business and lead the industry?
- Who are the team leaders in design, sales, and marketing who are responsible for making the project a market success?

- How have we staffed the key positions in design, marketing, and operations?

If we focus our discussions on these topics, we can define much smaller, faster-moving projects; have a much clearer sense of what will make the product valuable to our customers; and can approach all new products with a much greater sense of urgency. Perhaps most importantly, we will determine the makeup of the team with the right amount of due diligence and care.

Yet I must add, I am disappointed with the level of direction that I see between many of the general managers and their design teams. As you know, I am a great believer in Peter Drucker's management adage, "You only get what you inspect," and many GMs are simply not inspecting their R&D investments adequately. In fact, many have abdicated this responsibility to plant managers, many of whom continue to practice our old funding cycle process.

It's time for a dramatically new approach to managing our R&D projects. Our current processes of funding are stuck in our past, in a time period when markets were in our control.

However, that was the past. Now we are in an era where market windows are extremely short and unforgiving. This is the new world. What we must learn now is how to manage content and technological risk in order to hit the market window. Because hitting the market window is definitely *not* the focus of our step review process, *I am canceling it today.* I am taking this step to clear the way for the adoption of processes that are more appropriate for our future. The focus of the new process must be on marshaling the entire team's energy and knowledge to hit the market window with more value than our competition. To be late today means we are not a player in the market.

It's time to stop treating the technology resources as a functional silo or independent subcontractor, and instead view it as an integral part of each business unit. Rather than discuss funding for R&D projects at meeting after meeting, we need to address who we will assign to which projects.

Clearly, every new product development program must have a budget and a management process that is understood and followed by every member of the new product commercialization effort. I also recognize that our business units serve different markets and face different competitors, so as we move away from the old review process I do not expect to replace it with a one-size-fits-all corporatewide process. What I expect instead is adherence to sound management principles and judgment by our GMs and executive team. Some specifics of my expectations are as follows:

- Because the GM is ultimately responsible for the success of all R&D investments, I expect the GMs to take a personal interest in their top five projects. In particular, I expect they will help the team prioritize and freeze the product definition and technology approach.

- I expect the GM to hand pick the individuals that staff their critical new product developments, and ensure that the team members' authority and responsibilities are clearly understood. I also expect the GM to be easily accessible to the leaders of their top projects.
- I expect the GM at the outset to define project success for the team in *market* terms. We also need to set dates that we all relate to—it's time to set real calendar dates such as July 15th, rather than the old factory dates of "week 49," which mean absolutely nothing to our external customers.
- The real success for the project team is not just hitting milestones, but achieving revenue, orders, and margin objectives. At the same time, let's recognize that not all bets will succeed, and rather than penalize our innovators for projects that don't pan out, let's encourage them to try again.
- Let's ensure that our design resources are fully integrated into our business units. Although it's been 2 years since we moved the reporting lines of our development teams from our centralized structure to the business units, my sense is that for the most part we still operate as though the technical resources are part of a separate organization. It's time to stop treating these valuable resources as a functional silo.
- Let's ensure we have the communications processes, vehicles, and resources in place to quickly share with all employees our major contract wins and losses. To instill a "customer-one" culture, everyone needs to understand the significance of the win, which competitors we beat, and why the customers chose NBx. At the same time, everyone needs to know why we lost a contract, what the loss means to the corporation, and what we could have done differently. *Let's debrief both successes and losses.*

I am now taking the first step in this area by, as I mentioned earlier, canceling our step review process, a process I actually introduced in 1985 when I was the president of ExT. I introduced the process at a time when our software releases had doubled in size, and we were struggling to regain control of the quality and schedules of the loads we were shipping to our large installed base. Over the years, however, the step review process evolved to become the corporate standard and has been applied to every development project, regardless of the project's size or complexity. Unfortunately, my sense is that the reviews are no longer being used as a mechanism to ensure we hit our schedule, but rather as an opportunity to redefine the schedule, which results in us missing our market commitments.

We must now use every dollar we spend to make NBx stronger: to give us a stronger product portfolio, to build customer loyalty, to help achieve our goal of being the most valued company in the industry (by customers, employees, shareholders, and communities), to make our people more productive, and/or to put more money into the people and resources needed to ensure we release our projects in the shortest amount of time. The focus of the process must be one of absolute determination to overcome all obstacles and beat the competition for our customers' business.

I also expect the GM and the project team to have a set of clearly defined criteria for shutting down a project that falls behind schedule. Our current practice of continual redirections and extensions is no longer acceptable.

I believe each of you are up the challenge, a challenge to move as fast as our competitors and to let our software designers feel the full excitement of the marketplace.

Discussion Questions

1. Select statements from Joan Rivers that you identify as intellectually stimulating, inspirational, and individually considerate. Indicate reasons for your choices.
2. Select statements that reflect constructive contingent rewards and corrective active managing by exception and passive managing by exception. Could any of these statements be reframed more positively?
3. How would you react to Joan's abandonment of the step review process?
4. What do you think Joan's next acts should be in the transformation that has been initiated by eliminating the step review process?

21

Back to the Past When the Future Seemed So Obvious*

Many organizations have been making the effort to reengineer their structure to increase efficiency and effectiveness. One of the predominant efforts has been to introduce integrated information technology systems such as enterprise resource planning (ERP) to integrate communications and database systems within organizations. This case examines the outlook toward the implementation of an ERP in three different organizations. In the first instance, the organization was thinking about how to restructure the business to compete and excel in the next 5 to 10 years. The use of technology and an ERP was not the focus, but instead a secondary item in restructuring the organization's direction. The second company reviewed the potential of an ERP and found it to be overwhelming. They believed that they would never be able to predict the future, and therefore they would not be able to make concrete decisions about the adoption of an ERP. They decided not to adopt an ERP and instead to "go with the flow." The third organization had become fat over the past years and was unresponsive to market signals. The organization spent 6 months discussing the adoption of an ERP because the team was focused on cost savings. After 9 months, the system still had not been implemented because the organization's culture was resistant to change. The final decision was to rewrite code for the ERP so that it better fit the current structure. This alteration would extend the project by several months and increase costs.

Over the last 5 years, a dramatic revolution has been occurring in organizations around the world. Part of the revolution is stimulated by the whole effort to reengineer organizations for optimal efficiency and effectiveness. Building on the global wave of reengineering efforts, there has been a dra-

---

*An original case written by the editors.

matic change occurring in organizations with the introduction of integrated information technology systems such as enterprise resource planning (ERP). These systems provide a fully integrated platform for all of the communication and database systems within organizations, and they are now beginning to dramatically affect the way work is completed in those organizations that have changed to a new integrated information system. If you change communication frameworks in organizations, you change relationships. If you change relationships, you change the structure of organizations. If you change the structure, you inevitably change the leadership system and its functions.

Integrated information technology systems such as ERP have the ability to dramatically change the way we organize work flow processes, and can place organizations well into the future in terms of their relationships with employees, customers, suppliers, and global markets. There are many ways that an organization can approach the integration of new technology, which may also say a great deal about its leadership. Let's review some examples of how three organizations dealt with the introduction of an ERP system.

Look Far Forward

When the leadership of the first organization was examining the purchase of an ERP system, they were also thinking ahead 5 to 10 years about how the organization should be restructured, what markets it should be pursuing, the information it would need to be ahead of its customers' desires, and the type of culture needed to support the organization's future workforce. ERP was seen as a secondary item with respect to these discussions. Often, as the future was laid out in these discussions, the leaders would stop and ask, "Can ERP support that?" The use of technology was not the future target point in their discussion—it was the means to support what they had envisioned for the "new organization" they were attempting to create. Treating ERP as a secondary issue was quite a challenge, in that it was the single biggest investment in technology that had ever been made by this company in its 30-year history.

Don't Look, Just Do

In the second organization, executives sat around the table reading the specs on the ERP system. They were clearly impressed with its capabilities, but as one executive said, "How do we get from where we are, in terms of our organization's structure, to where this technology can place us in the future?" This question surfaced many times during the meetings on whether to adopt ERP, and each time no concrete answers were provided. The system and its capabilities seemed to be so overwhelming for the group to even consider that they didn't consider them at all! Prior to making the final adoption decision, the senior executive on the team concluded, "We will never be able to predict exactly which way this tornado will turn, so therefore I suggest we go with the flow and maintain an open mind." All present agreed.

Look Far Back

In the third organization, there was a great deal of change going on prior to any discussion of ERP. The organization had become fat and happy with its success, and was now so insulated from its markets, that it rarely heard what customers had to say about its products. The organization was starting to receive signals from the market that its strategy and products were falling behind the competition. Outside the company, the market was shifting dramatically and competition was picking up. Inside the company, the birds were still singing and the air was calm and warm. Nothing seemed to be happening that would suggest that this organization was coming toward a huge cliff!

Being largely comprised of engineers and computer scientists, this organization was frequently looking to adopt new technology. Over the last 9 months, they had made the decision to adopt and implement ERP. The deliberations around this decision were primarily based on the cost savings associated with moving to an ERP system. However, 6 months into the process, they were confronting tremendous resistance in their corporate culture to implementing ERP. The implementation of ERP had barely progressed over a 6-month period, and costs for implementation were mounting. Three months later, a senior executive from the technologies division finally called a meeting to indicate there was a problem that he felt needed to be addressed. With the implementation of ERP hung up, many other systems were facing uncertainty, and this senior executive felt that down the road this would likely affect the ability to compete in its current markets.

After some discussion, the group decided that they would ask the ERP technicians to rewrite some of the code so that it fit better into the organization's current structure and processes. The senior executive and his team seemed satisfied with this "fix" of the problem, even though it would delay implementation several months and cost an additional 15% of the original purchase price for the ERP. However, as one executive said, "I'd rather rewrite some code than try to change our culture." The others laughed in agreement, and said, "That's a no-brainer!"

Discussion Questions

1. Can you explain the differences among the three organizations in terms of the full range of leadership model?

2. How would you make use of the best thinking that occurred in each of the three organizations?

3. What are some strategies that you could use to take advantage of implementing an ERP system for culture change?

4. How similar are the situations described in this case to situations you have been personally involved with? How did people in those situations react to the change process?

5. Is there a fourth approach that would be best, or at least better?

22

Amy's Debrief*

NTC Medical Supplies Corporation had been stagnant—sometimes declining—for years. At this year's management retreat, the CEO, Bob, decided that the organization was troubled and he wanted to express his concern and encourage managers to make a turnaround. His message was for managers to "ignite the troops" and "drive business growth." Bob even quoted financial goals for the end of the year. However, the executives seemed to be unresponsive. Bob was not clear about what changes should be made and how they should be implemented. Furthermore, after receiving little feedback from those attending the retreat, Bob discovered that the reason no one showed passion was that the organizational culture discouraged initiative and innovation. Amy, a young executive, shared an experience when her proposal for a new project prompted other managers to disparage her, and ultimately hurt her career. The culture at NTC rewarded status quo and punished innovation.

It was the yearly meeting of the whole global senior management team for the NTC Medical Supplies Corporation. NTC was a high-tech company that produced specialty products for surgical procedures. Every year the management board got together for half a day to discuss next year's upcoming strategy, and then went to play golf for the next three and a half days. Year after year it was the same pattern, where the senior executives treated themselves to royal treatment while the company sailed like the *Titanic* toward disaster.

This year, however, things were a bit different. The head of the human resources (HR) department realized that the company was on course for di-

---

*An original case written by the editors.

saster, and was working with Bob, the CEO, on how to make changes in the way their company operated. Bob was well aware that business was not where it should be, and he was now committed to pushing his management team to drive business growth at double-digit rates. Their stock value had been flat all throughout the greatest bull market of all time! Something was terribly wrong with this company's picture. Unfortunately, no one knew exactly what Bob meant by "drive business growth," nor were they compelled to do so in any consistent fashion. Bob's top senior management team had become complacent in their past success. One young manager described the situation best: "The furniture and the mindsets around here are both stuck in the 1970s."

The retreat started with Bob giving his opening speech, which he had prepared to "ignite the troops." He really tried to be inspiring, but each time he painted a positive picture of what could be, he slid back to complaining about NTC's poor performance, and how they just weren't "growing the business." Bob wanted them to increase NTC's stock value, but was very short on specifics, except to repeat again and again the financial goals for the year. He honestly felt that his job was to clarify the end goal, and the managers' jobs were to make it happen.

By the end of Bob's speech, he had alienated most of the executives in the room, except some very loyal sycophants who kept saying, "You know, Bob has a good point, blah, blah, blah!"

The group broke for the evening feeling very disillusioned. The next morning a famous leadership guru spoke to them for 3 hours, giving them all sorts of examples about the new "organizational order" out there. Each time he stopped to dialogue with the audience, he got blank stares. He turned on his way out of the room before lunch, and said to Bob under his breath, "They got no damn passion!"

In the afternoon session, the group received 360° feedback. The feedback was on their leadership styles, and it is fair to say that for some the results weren't pretty. Many thought they were much better leaders than they actually were based on follower, peer, and supervisory ratings. This is not an uncommon overestimation in leadership feedback lore. The group started to see they were not the *ideal* leaders they perceived themselves to be. The areas they collectively received the worst ratings in were *coaching* their followers, and in spending too much time on *searching for mistakes*. Again, the people in the room were not at their most inspired moment, and it is fair to say they had no damn passion!

Bob asked to address the audience before they broke for the afternoon. He told them about the comment from the leadership guru that morning, and said, "We must instill passion in each other. Let's seize this opportunity based on our feedback to do things differently. Could the ratings be a wake-up call?" Bob desperately needed the manager's assertiveness, and asked them to stop looking to him for all of the leadership in this company. It was time for them to come to the table. Bob then asked, "Does anyone have anything to say, any feedback at all for me?"

No one moved, so he went to sit down. Just then, the HR director stood up and said, "Now isn't there anyone here who has an opinion he or she would like to share with Bob? Anyone? He just asked you for feedback." A young woman by the name of Amy said she would like to address the group. She said that 3 years ago, when she was at her first senior management retreat, the company's then-COO asked her to present a new project initiative. He had really pumped her up to present this new project to the senior management group, but neglected to tell her about the strong resistance in the group to launching the new project. She was the sacrificial lamb and was verbally torn apart by the group. Amy told Bob that she firmly believed that this experience at her first retreat had really hurt her career. Following that meeting, many of the managers referred to her as a "lightweight." Amy asked Bob why he didn't come to the table when leadership was needed back then to balance out the damage done to her. She was set up and he knew it!

An older lawyer in the group quickly jumped in and said, "Now Amy, you may be overreacting a bit, and didn't you get that promotion you wanted last year anyhow? Maybe you're being a little too emotional." Essentially, the lawyer was implying that Amy was being a little too female in a group of senior managers who were primarily males who played golf together whether they enjoyed it or not. In actuality Amy wasn't at all being emotional, but that was the lawyer's limited interpretation. Bob sat listening and then said, "Amy, I am sorry, because it did hurt your career and I should have intervened but didn't. I was in a terrible fight with the COO before he finally left, and chose not to engage him that day. You have a right to be angry with me. I'm sorry. It won't happen again."

At that point, a young manager from Italy spoke up. He said that his general manager had cautioned him before his first senior management meeting "to not say anything interesting, got it, nothing interesting." There was some nervous laughter around the room, and then it appeared that people began to realize the implications of getting 42 managers from the farthest points around the world together for 4 days at the Ritz-Carlton not to say anything interesting. How interesting.

Discussion Questions

1. Please describe how Bob handled this retreat in terms of his leadership style. Also, identify other events and incidents in this case that denote effective and/or ineffective leadership and followership.

2. If you were in the audience, how would you take on the challenge being presented by Bob and the HR director?
3. What did you learn from this case regarding how to debrief events that have an impact on your followers' perceptions of you as a leader?
4. What should be Bob's next steps in the follow-up retreat that he scheduled for 2 months after the annual retreat?

23

A Doll's House*

When Jill Elikann Barad was appointed CEO of Mattel, she initiated moves to un-load noncore businesses and abandoned a longstanding emphasis on double-digit quarterly earnings growth. Described by colleagues as a hard-driving manager with an instinct for what kids like, Barad won early recognition for reenergizing Barbie, the doll that represented $1.7 billion of Mattel's $3.8 billion 1996 annual revenue. (Nevertheless, she was ousted as CEO after several years in office.) This case reviews Barad's background, and includes an interview conducted while she was still Mattel's CEO.

Is Mattel Ready for a Makeover?

When Jill Elikann Barad, 46, was appointed to succeed John Amerman, who had run the El Segundo, CA, toymaker for 10 years, she initiated moves to unload non-core businesses and abandoned a long-standing emphasis on double-digit quarterly earnings growth—a hallmark of her predecessor, who continues as chairman. Described by colleagues as a hard-driving manager with an instinct for what kids like, Barad won early recognition for re-energizing Barbie, the 11.5-inch doll that currently represents $1.7 billion of Mattel's $3.8 billion 1996 annual revenue.

Like Amerman, who had also been president of Mattel's international unit prior to becoming CEO, Barad faced short-term financial reverses that led to restructuring charges, including layoffs, the phasing out of non-performing assets, and the streamlining of international operations. Cur-

---

*Donlon, J. P. (1997). A doll's house. *Chief Executive, 127*, 32–36. (Adapted)

rent challenges relate to the merger with Tyco Toys, weakness in European sales, and a major decline in Fisher-Price products—a line the company acquired more than a year ago.

The company also took a bruising in the media for its failed merger attempt with Hasbro. Between 1988 and 1996, Mattel had achieved a compound annual growth rate of 18 percent in revenue and 34 percent in income before charges. The company projects 7 percent revenue growth this year. While Mattel's cash position—more than $500 million last year—is strong, Barad's immediate charge is improving topline growth, which is down to 4 percent on an annualized basis. She must also depart from Mattel's former business practices. Several large toy retailers last year warned Mattel and other toy makers that they will no longer sanction the industry practice of shipping merchandise above previously agreed levels at quarter's end to boost sales targets.

The Brooklyn-born and Long Island-bred Barad, who earlier in her career created such Barbie variations as Teen Talk Barbie, Barbie Businesswoman, and, more recently, an interactive Barbie complete with CD-ROM, has no doubt that she is up to the task of reinventing Mattel. She plans to focus on global brand building, emphasizing the four core brands—Barbie, Hot Wheels, Fisher-Price, and Disney licenses—that represent 87 percent of revenue. In fact, on the day CE [*Chief Executive* magazine] visited with Barad, Mattel execs in the next office were conferring with a close-cropped Demi Moore about adding yet another new face to the Barbie Bunch—Barbie Planet Hollywood. Meanwhile, the remaining 13 percent of Mattel product lines are to be vetted for worldwide appeal, profitability, and what Barad calls "sustainable play pattern"—the success of a particular toy or toy genre to capture children's imagination.

In fact, rather than compare Mattel with other toy companies, Barad would prefer to have it likened to a consumer brand company on the order of a Gillette or a P&G—a thought not completely discounted by Mattel observers. "When you look at companies like Gillette and P&G, their businesses are not as seasonal as Mattel's and their world markets are perceived as being a lot bigger, so I don't know that Mattel will get to that point of comparison," says an industry analyst. "However, from an earnings, growth, and consistency standpoint, they have accomplished a lot and can be considered a very inexpensive consumer stock."

Like those on her executive team—such as Bruce Stein, president of Mattel Worldwide, who returned to the company after a stint with Hasbro's Kenner Toys—Barad is viewed as a product person able to hone in on the strength or weakness of a product. Her ability to recognize a product as "toyetic"—a highly developed skill—will be increasingly put to the test as the company pushes for growth in tough international markets—and corresponding local product differentiation. An Angel Princess doll considered acceptable in North America and the U.K., for example, is borderline sacrilegious in Catholic Italy and Spain.

Barad began her career first as a model, then dropped out of college to sell Love Cosmetics. She returned to New York City's Queens College to graduate in 1973 with degrees in English and psychology. After flirting with the idea of becoming an actress, she took a trainee position at Coty Cosmetics and was later promoted to marketing positions at the company, where she met her husband, movie producer Tom Barad, and moved to Los Angeles. There she worked in advertising on the Max Factor account before leaving to have the first of two sons. Barad joined Mattel in 1981 as a product manager. As she climbed the ranks from within, one of her tasks was to rejuvenate the image of Barbie, whose sales were beginning to flatten. Her success brought her to the attention of then Mattel chairman Arthur Spear. After being named president of the girls and activity toys divisions, she was named president of Mattel USA in 1990 and COO in 1992. As the sole woman CEO in the Fortune 500 (Golden West Financial's Marion Sanders shares the title with her husband), Barad has become a high-profile executive. But while companies and recruiters call her weekly to join their boards, she's adamant about limiting herself to three outside boards: Microsoft, BankAmerica, and Pixar. When told she is sometimes described as difficult to work for, Barad exhibits a range of expressiveness to rival Lucille Ball's, rolling her eyes as if to say "they can't be talking about me." "I want to get the best from people," she responds, eyes widening in mock horror.

Unabashedly declaring that her family comes first, Barad says more companies should judge people on performance and not whether they are 18-hour-day office drones. Her own goal is to make Mattel a fun place to work. Recalling a business trip to Las Vegas where several members of senior management had 20 minutes to kill before their return flight to Los Angeles, a senior executive recounts how Mattel's CEO disappeared briefly, returning to distribute coins for the airport slot machines. "We're a toy company. We're supposed to have fun," she quips.

Q: You took over Mattel in the wake of the Tyco merger. What were the most critical business challenges you faced?

A: Last year, we had a softening of the top line that threw us off and the outside world off in terms of their confidence in us. The biggest issue was regaining Mattel's credibility as a consumer products company in the business of building global power brands versus a toy company in the business of finding this year's hot new toy. I needed to get everybody focused again on the fact that we were building global power brands and get the merger with Tyco done. Our brands already had great appeal across the world, but in certain countries we lacked the organization, the infrastructure, the relationships, and the distribution ability we have today. So we needed more brands to do the brand building that we do so well, and we needed to do it in more places than ever before.

Q: What did you address first?

A: I had to fix a brand issue that resulted from a strategic misstep. Fisher-Price, which had a great reputation for quality, decided that they should go into every category that was being sold to children from zero to five. This was at a time of excitement about educational and electronic learning toys, which were outside our core expertise. So we entered those categories and didn't add anything new to our core holdings. I spent a lot of time getting them back on track.

Then we changed the strategic underpinnings to focus on basic but innovative traditional infant and preschool products. We managed out of the other businesses and brought the infant and preschool brands of Mattel together. Today, Mattel is $1.6 billion in infant and preschool brands, almost equal to Barbie. We have the hottest licenses, with sustainable characters that are well established.

Q: What changes did the Tyco merger and the restructuring bring?

A: With the addition of Matchbox and Tyco, we now have $500 million in the wheels business. And Matchbox's name recognition outside the U.S. helped our international vision. Now we're asking, "What can we do to innovate the way they're distributed? The way they are merchandised? The way they're created? The way they're developed?" We decided to sell Matchbox in vending machines; you put in $1 and the car drives down a lane and falls into the little boy's hand. We want to develop each of these businesses so they can be seen as standalone companies. That should allow us sustainable, consistent growth year after year around the world.

Q: Your share price is at an all time high, yet last March you indicated annual growth of 7 percent, which is below your pattern. What are your forecasts?

A: We said 7 percent for this year only because of the effect of the dollar. Going forward, it would be 10 percent on the top line, 15 percent on the bottom line. We give a projection for the year and then talk five and 10 years out because I want people behind us who are in for

the long haul. We are still undervalued compared to the companies—
not toy companies, but companies like P&G and General Foods—that
we would put ourselves against.

You can't really put us in a category with toy competitors because
our main competitor is nothing like us. They're in the licensed toy
business. They're looking for that hot property and they change it every year. We're more about brand building. Barbie has been around
for 38 years now, and she grew 20 percent in her 37th year. Hot
Wheels virtually doubled this year already, and now we also have
Matchbox. So we need to compare ourselves with other peer consumer products companies in the business of building brands. And
those are not necessarily toy companies.

Q: What are your goals for growing Mattel's international business?

A: To grow it to 60 percent of earnings over the next five years. We are
trying to make our international operations far more efficient, so that
we have even greater margin opportunities outside the U.S. For example, in Europe we utilize 35 warehouses. We'd like to go down to
two.

We are aligning ourselves strategically with some of the best dis-
tributors in the world and taking advantage of their clout. We have
signed a deal with Avon, which has some of the best direct selling distribution both in and outside the U.S., particularly in developing
countries. When our retailers go into these countries, we'll be poised
and ready.

Q: What other international moves are you making?

A: We've hired outside consultants. We've worked long and hard to
open the door to Japan. We had been operating there through a li-
cense agreement, so we hadn't done the necessary research. When
we took over, we went in and spent time with kids. We've seen tremendous results in the last six to eight months because we finally realized that there is a different play pattern that goes on there. Little
girls in the U.S. dream about what they will be when they grow up,
and little girls in Japan dream about what they are today. Our line reflects both, but in the U.S. we play up the part about dreaming about
being a doctor or an astronaut. So we cut out that part for Japan and
focused on the everyday stuff. Once we did that, sales took off.

Q: At some consumer companies, the brand has at one time or another
been considered sacred—any extension or modification was almost a
sacrilege. Has that ever been an issue at Mattel?

A: If you understand your brand, there's no limit to the creativity that you can have. All of the limits to what everybody felt Barbie was or could ever be were blown apart in the last 15 years. The last time CE wrote about Mattel, the whole company was at $1 billion in revenue. Barbie alone will be $2 billion this year. So I believe that having a formula for something is the worst thing in the world, because any formula can be copied. It's not fresh. It's not new. And it's not making you stretch your thinking.

You have to look at two real factors in a brand very often. How relevant you are and how differentiated you are from everything else out there. The more predictable you become, the more vulnerable you are.

Q: How has Barbie changed?

A: She has evolved just as everyone else has evolved. We're in the fashion business in a sense. People aren't buying what Barbie was 10 years ago. They want to know why Barbie's relevant today. Barbie's a reflection of what's going on with today's girls, and that changes every year.

Last year she had all new joints and could move for the first time, and this year she's able to walk. It's in a low-tech manner, because Barbie will retail for only about $5.12. You hold her waist and she walks across the table. Barbie can talk this year, and she actually uses your name and talks about things relevant to you. You point your mouse to particular icons in a special CD program and it downloads immediately into her and stores that information. So when your best friend comes over, she'll say, "Hey Glenn!"

Q: How do you decide to let Barbie do this or that?

A: We test with kids and moms around the world. Sometimes, it's when I feel, "Oh God, that's really scary," that those are the best ideas. A good illustration is Share a Smile Becky, Barbie's new best friend who is in a wheelchair. Maybe some people would have said that was inappropriate. But response has been unbelievable. It's been out for about three months and we sold out. It's being bought not only by the specially abled community but the entire mass market community.

We're not necessarily here to educate. But if we can open up a child's thinking about the world, why not? We had Teacher Barbie last year, and she had ethnically diverse students. She came with two students, and every package had a different mix of students, because that's the real world. Students come in lots of colors. We feel a responsibility to get girls where we think the world is going.

Q: Guys and dolls. How do you respond to critics who say that toy manufacturers sexually stereotype children?

A: Boys always show more aggressive play. Give them pots, and they'll slam them against the floor. A girl will explore what's inside and treat it with care. There are clear gender play patterns. What we want children to play with and to like has nothing to do with where their tastes are. If you put 30 colors up there, a little girl most often will pick pink, red, or purple. I didn't do anything to make her do that. A boy will pick blue, yellow, or green. And that is reflected in toys.

Q: What is Mattel doing to enhance its position with little boys?

A: Hot Wheels, Matchbox, and Tyco RC are $500 million today. We expect that to reach $1 billion within the next three or four years. These are boys' toys that will be around for years to come. I don't want to be in the game of having some hot licensed property that brings in $300 million next year and then the following year have to replace $300 million in business.

Q: As the mother of two sons, what do you feel boys look for in toys?

A: Barbie changes dramatically from year to year depending on girls' tastes. It's the same thing with boys. This year they're into space, with Star Wars, and some years they're under sea or into Westerns. I would love to have the boys' counterpart to Barbie—not a Barbie for boys, but a character that we can grow and nurture and change and have reflect boys as they change. My two sons prefer computer games.

Q: How has the shift toward software affected the toy business?

A: We are in software development already. Barbie Fashion Designer was the No. 1 selling new software introduction last year. We're looking into it in our other businesses. We can use that medium to actually bring boys and girls back to us in a dynamic way. We'll be able to have a car designed by a boy on his computer uploaded to us, so that we can give him a 3D model of it. There's no question that interactivity will be the way of the world.

Q: When developing Disney products, how do you factor in the risk associated with a given character's lifespan?

A: When we just did one movie for Disney, we were very dependent on the outcome of that movie. But the new relationship that we just signed with Disney last year gave us the rights to all their properties. With Hercules, retail response wasn't strong from the outset, but we also had all the other Disney characters. So we saw 14 percent growth in our Disney business in the U.S. during the Hercules launch.

Q: What is your management style?

A: I try to do things with humor and a sense of fun versus an iron fist. I don't believe in firing people for mistakes. I've made mistakes in my career and I'm still here. I rally everyone together and say, "Let's look at it in a different way." It's people's sense of their own importance in a company that keeps them motivated. We could all do amazing things if we believe that others thought we were good enough.

The worst thing someone can do is clone themselves. What we're comfortable with is what we know, so we end up duplicating ourselves. It's a real problem in management today. If you want to screw up your business, that's the best way—to have all the same personality types with the same vision and the same expertise.

Q: How do you balance work and family?

A: Period. I don't miss a single birthday, whether it's a board meeting or the world coming to an end. There were times when I thought that would turn everybody off. When I was pregnant, I thought that was pretty much the end of my career, and that's when I got promoted to director of Barbie. That's what gave me enough confidence to not feel threatened. I wouldn't compromise my children for anything.

Q: What advice would you give firms trying to find the Barads in their companies?

A: Judge people on performance. They should be able to perform their jobs in the time it takes to do a job. Don't make people work 18 hours and judge them because their bodies are there. You want people with balance in their lives. I feel strongly about quality-of-life issues. Talent is the name of the game here. People develop toys. People manufacture toys. People market toys. And if we're going to get the best of them, we've got to start thinking about their total lives.

I want our people to get out of the four walls of this building and experience more in their lives so that they bring it back here. We have half days on Fridays. This year, I gave everyone four fun Fridays off and 16 days off for Christmas, versus 12 last year. And our people get two extra days to go see their kids at school. We just announced extended family benefits, so that you can cover an extra dependent.

We put in a child-care facility and a gym and went to casual dress instead of formal attire. We're a toy company. We're supposed to have fun. We shouldn't look like bankers.

Discussion Questions

1. How does Barad's style of leadership differ from other leaders about whom you have read?
2. What are some aspects of her style of leadership that you feel you could adopt in your own style?
3. How do you think this CEO's style would work in DaimlerChrysler? GM? Why?
4. Why do you think Barad was ousted eventually, and how might her demise have been avoided?

IV

ETHICAL ISSUES

Many people regard the term *business ethics* as an oxymoron, suggesting that we can practice one or the other but not both. The truth is that to be a transformational leader one must set an example of what it means to be morally correct, just, fair, and open, and to do what is good and right. One may be guided by ethical principles of what is just, what is right, and what is good, or one may be guided by the expected consequences of actions (e.g., will they be harmful or beneficial to others?). The cases in Part IV are as follows:

24. Managerial Ethical Leadership: Adrian Cadbury
25. Jim Corby
26. The Commandant's Dilemma
27. Jack Gets a Grip
28. The Fine Art of Leadership

24

Managerial Ethical Leadership:
Adrian Cadbury*

*The central role of corporate leaders in setting the ethical tone for their organiza-
tion is widely accepted. Cadbury Schweppes CEO Adrian Cadbury is profiled in
this case to illustrate how his managerial ethical leadership influenced not only his
firm but also the practice of business. Cadbury always focused on building personal relationships within the firm. The two characteristics he most emphasized
were fairness and openness, which are important for upholding ethical business
practices. Cadbury even developed methods to help managers make ethical
choices in business decisions.*

George Adrian Hayhurst Cadbury was born in 1929 and educated at Eton
and King's College at Cambridge University. He was the fourth generation of
his Quaker family to head Cadbury Schweppes, the maker of chocolate
products and beverages. He became CEO in 1969 and aggressively pushed
the firm into international markets including the United States. His management style emphasized decentralized decision-making.

This move into the international arena forced the company to adapt to
the culture of different countries. Cadbury Schweppes has a tradition of
strong worker participation and they try to involve people in their subsidiary
companies in decision-making. [Cadbury] pushed all top executives to spend
some time traveling to various plant locations and building personal relationships within the firm. According to Cadbury, "In the end, the glue that holds
the company together is the personal contact and a belief that the company
stands for something worthwhile and to spread the shared values."

---

*Murphy, P., & Enderle, G. (1995). Managerial ethical leadership: Examples do matter.
Business Ethics Quarterly, 5(1), 117–118. (Adapted)

Two characteristics of Cadbury Schweppes that he emphasized were fairness and openness. The firm has developed a reputation for fairness in the normally hostile British labor environment and provided complete information to various power groups. This fairness extended beyond employee issues to acquisitions and divestment. The company would only acquire a firm if it could function better as part of the company. Similarly, the firm spun off its UK Food Group when the subsidiary argued that it could operate better as a separate company. Sir Adrian strongly advocated openness: "But I believe in the principle that you should manage in an open way: tell people what is going on and listen to what they have to offer, particularly when it concerns matters which affect them very directly." He also included openness as one of the eight guiding characteristics of the firm.

In an article that could be labeled a primer on ethical management, Cadbury outlined his philosophical position on a number of ethical issues business. He offered many sage words in this treatise and attributed the ethical values that pervade his firm to his grandfather. According to Cadbury the ethical standards of a company are judged by its actions rather than statements of good intentions. In making management decisions, Cadbury uses a two-step process: first to determine what our personal rules of conduct are and second to think through who else will be affected by the decision and how we should weight their interest in it.

To deal with one of the most difficult ethical issues facing managers in the international arena (how far to go in buying business), Cadbury uses two simple rules of thumb. Is the payment on the face of the invoice? Would it embarrass the recipient to have the gift mentioned in the company newspaper? The first test makes certain that all payments are recorded and "on the books." The second, which is a version of *The Wall Street Journal* test, is aimed at distinguishing bribes from gifts. The logic behind these rules is that openness and ethics go together. He indicates that openness is the "best way to disarm outside suspicion of the companies' motives and actions." Cadbury retired from his position at Cadbury Schweppes in 1990, but his influence on ethical management practices in the UK continued. He has been involved in Business in the Community to encourage the formation of new enterprises with a sense of social responsibility. Most recently, he headed the influential Cadbury Commission which reported on corporate governance and methods for placing outside directors on Boards to insure that they can provide an independent voice regarding management decisions.

Discussion Questions

1. Is Cadbury merely an exception to the rule in his focus on the need for fairness, openness, and candor in business?

2. How does Cadbury illustrate that leaders who display aspects of full range leadership can do so with a strong sense of what is right and the importance for a manager to be ethical?

3. If you were a Cadbury Schweppes salesperson in a country known for the buyers' expectations of bribery, what would you do?

4. If you were a purchasing agent for Cadbury Schweppes in the same country and were offered a bonus to close the deal, what would you do?

25

Jim Corby*

One of the most important aspects of leadership is establishing credibility. To do this, leaders need to be transparent and to consistently exhibit high moral and ethical leadership. How difficult it is to establish such standards is portrayed in the following case.

At lunch the other day, we were talking about our last supervisor, Jim Corby, who left the company last year. Three years earlier, he had been hired to work as a member of a team of circuit board assemblers. After a short time on the job, he showed his technical competence with an initiative that helped members of other teams as well as his team's performance. He did small favors for his teammates and kept on the best of terms with Jane Taliaferro, the team supervisor at that time. He usually kept his complaints to himself before unloading on his best friend. Jim was quick to agree with Jane, his supervisor—sometimes too quick. At the meetings of the team before starting a new assignment, he stayed out of controversies, was careful in what he said, seldom disagreed with majority opinion, and generally made a good impression.

When Jane was transferred, Jim was given the position even though he had less seniority than some of the others considered for the job. Some people thought it was due to his technical competence; others said it was because he was always trying to butter up the managers at our monthly meetings with them.

---

*An original case written by the editors.

Jim thought he was a pretty good supervisor. He was a fairly likeable guy, but for one reason or another, we had found him hard to trust. We tried to figure out why. We decided that although he appeared to do the right things, often he was deceiving both himself and us. For instance, he talked a lot about the moral thing to do, yet he insisted on doing whatever it took to keep the director happy, including brushing over mistakes. Jim would act like we had just received an emergency request, and get us all hot and bothered to stop everything else to handle the matter, when in fact the request was actually a routine one. When he said that he would set us an example by working after hours, he actually seldom stayed late.

He often was flattering for trivialities when he thought he was praising someone for an important, well-done job. He was quick to make promises that we learned he couldn't keep. He took our failures personally as if we intentionally didn't try hard enough so he would get "mud on his face." He talked about getting a bonus for all of us, but only three of us got bonuses and he got one himself that was twice as much as ours.

He asked to be trusted and told us a lot of what we liked to hear. Only after he left did we find out that some of what he had said was misleading. He talked a lot about empowering and delegating, but in fact kept us on a tight leash whenever something that had to be done was important.

When we were trying to reorganize for a new mission, his suggestions were stimulating but his arguments were oversimplified, based on false assumptions and half-truths. What authorities had said was more important to him than reason. Although he appeared sympathetic when we approached him with problems at work or home, his behavior indicated a lack of concern (withdrawing, changing the subject, not listening, etc.). Instead of being supportive, he was ingratiating and quick to turn the meeting into a discussion of his problems.

Discussion Questions

1. What is the evidence that Jim Corby was pseudoinspirational? Pseudointellectually stimulating? Pseudoindividually considerate?
2. Was Jim truly unethical, or was he unaware that he was pseudotransformational and pseudotransactional in his leadership rather than transformational and transactional?

26

The Commandant's Dilemma*

Lieutenant General Daniel W. Christman, U.S. Military Academy Commandant, was faced with a unique situation concerning the no-marriage rule. The commandant sent out an e-mail to inform others about the situation and the resolution of the dilemma. Two cadets were married while enrolled in the Academy. This was a violation that would result in expulsion from the institution. In this case, the cadets had the marriage annulled before any course of action was taken against them. The cadets were no longer subject to legal action because the marriage never legally existed. The commandant wanted to make others aware that the no-marriage rule was still intact and that these cadets were not given special treatment. He claimed he had made a judgment call and that he stood by his decision.

Background

The West Point Military Academy has a strict policy on not allowing married cadets to be enrolled in the institution. This is a longstanding policy of the institution. In the past, if the institution found out that a cadet had violated this regulation, that student would have been forced to leave the school.

Recently, a situation arose that stretched the policy to its extreme. Two cadets at the institution who were both enrolled in the academy had gotten married. This was discovered when one of the cadets indicated on the graduation form that the two were married. Thus, by telling the truth on the form, there was no honor code violation.

Subsequent to finding out about the violation, the commandant indicated that he had initiated a formal inquiry into the situation. The inquiry

---

*An original case written by the editors.

confirmed that the cadets were indeed married. While the forms to expel the cadets were being processed, the cadets had their marriage annulled. Because they were technically no longer married and in fact the marriage never existed, they could not be expelled, following the institution's own regulations. Many alumni of the institution reacted to these events with criticism of the decision not to expel. The attached e-mail from the commandant to a public network for alumni is his attempt to describe what occurred.

The memo is presented here verbatim.

To: West Point E-Mail Network

From: Commander

Subject: Policy on Married Cadets

Although we have made some earlier postings on the "married cadet" issue, many of you have asked for a recapitulation and a clarification of some key points. In an effort to be helpful, let me lay out some brief background data on the process, and then review the facts again. We obviously need to put this issue behind us, but at the same time I'm sensitive to the desire by you to understand more completely our rationale.

I'll start with the most basic point: I want to keep the "no marriage" policy intact. I believe in it, and don't want to see it changed. Despite all the letters and cyberspace traffic on this, it hasn't changed. What's changed is the way we separate cadets; it's changed a great deal from my day and when many of you graduated. Let me explain. First, separations are not automatic, nor have they been in recent times. They all require some "due process" for the individuals involved. Further, the amount of due process required by the Secretary of the Army has grown significantly. Since 1986, that "due process" has guaranteed an informal investigation under Army Regulation 15-6. No Superintendent any more can simply throw a cadet out without extending this guarantee. Second, the policies concerning separations for marriage, child support obligation, and pregnancy have also changed. They provide the Superintendent and the Secretary with much needed flexibility in handling these cases; the changes also ensure that cadet separations can withstand legal scrutiny if challenged. This is extremely critical. That's the reality of the legal environment all of us are working in. We can't change that.

With that background, let me explain again what happened in the particular case. In accordance with Regulations for the U.S. Military Academy, the Commandant immediately initiated the required informal investigation after we received information that the two cadets may have been married. After this expeditious investigation confirmed the no honor violation involved here; in fact, this case came to light when one of the cadets answered a question about marital status truthfully. While I was processing my recommendation to the Secretary of the Army to separate, the cadets obtained an annulment of the marriage. The cadets filed for the annulment; Academy officials neither suggested nor had any role in their legal course of action. Once the court ordered the marriage annulled (prior to the completion of my separation recommendation to Washington), my Staff Judge Advocate advised that there was no longer a legal basis to separate the cadets for marriage. I confirmed this opinion in numerous discussions with other attorneys both in Washington and elsewhere. As we stated in our first note on this issue, an annulment voids the marriage from its inception; in the eyes of the law, a marriage never existed. Rather than forward a recommendation to separate from the Army that I knew would be rejected, I made the decision to retain the two cadets. The decision was mine and mine alone.

Many of you have asked about the form which all of us used to sign upon return from leave ("I am not married"). It is no longer required. It went away in 1973. On R-Day cadets do sign an affirmation confirming their marital status as "single." The affirmation also includes a statement acknowledging understanding that a cadet who marries prior to graduation will be separated. Although the annulment legally prevented us from separating them, it did not prevent us from punishing them for violating the USCC SOP (cadet regulations.) They were punished. The Cadet Honor Committee reviewed this case. Because the Honor Committee determined there was no violation of the code, there was no officer review of the case for honor.

Additionally, the service academies' pregnancy policy has received a great deal of attention as part of this case. It's complicated, but it's important you understand it. First, a cadet may choose to terminate the pregnancy; if so, no adverse consequences occur. Of course, military medical treatment facilities cannot provide an abortion. However, a pregnant cadet has two other choices: she may resign, or she may request medical leave, without pay, for up to one year. In the event the cadet chooses neither option, I am authorized to direct medical leave. A cadet who chooses medical leave may return to the Corps once she has resolved custodial responsibility for her child and has demonstrated medical fitness. If the cadet chooses to maintain custodial responsibility for her child, a different paragraph in Regulations for the U.S. Military Academy provides that she will be separated from the Academy. Similarly, a male cadet who chooses to maintain custodial responsibility for his child, or who has a court-ordered child support obligation, will be separated.

That's the way the pregnancy policy has been since it was published in 1980 by the Secretary of the Army in coordination with then Superintendent, General Goodpaster, and Army Chief of Staff, General E.C. Meyer. It was last reviewed by HQDA in 1995 and reaffirmed. The policy was established to afford cadets (just like female soldiers on active duty) the maximum number of options with respect to the pregnancy. Before this policy was changed, the fear existed that cadets would avoid necessary medical care or try to terminate the pregnancy by illegal or unsafe medical procedures in order to avoid separation. Surely, we don't want to return to those days. The ultimate choice is hers; the Academy has no say in the decision. Cadets are counseled concerning their options and the possible consequences of selecting the various options, including service obligation issues. In accordance with this policy, the cadet in this case had a child last year, resolved the custody issue, and returned to the Corps; she will graduate at a later date.

The bottom line of all of this is that marriage by cadets is still against the Regulations; it has been that way since 1835. This longstanding restriction is intact. Thayer is not "turning in his grave"; married cadets were permitted in his day! The annulment action, a different civil process in most jurisdictions, confronted us with a new challenge. We faced it the way I'd like to think you'd want us to: by focusing on our goal of keeping the "no marriage policy," while addressing the implications of the annulment itself on that policy. Since, following the annulment, no marriage ever existed legally, we felt strongly we couldn't sustain the separation. That was my call. I surely don't endorse the cadets' actions that led to this dilemma in the first place, but I was bound to uphold the regulations and laws that dictated the resolution.

Let me reemphasize to each of you that I will continue to make decisions here in the best interest of the Military Academy, based on my judgment of what is "right" for the Academy. I seek all the available information and best advice available. No one influenced or directed my decision, no one.

I hope you find this information helpful and informative. As a final point, let me emphasize that any commander, following an action or "incident" like this one, will conduct what we today call an "after-action review." We're doing that now. While I felt strongly we couldn't separate the cadets under existing laws and regulations, we're examining carefully how these and associated procedures might be changed in the future to reinforce the "no marriage" policy. We'll keep you apprised.

Daniel W. Christman
Lieutenant General, U.S. Army Superintendent

Discussion Questions

1. Review the memo and examine how you felt the commandant dealt with the situation in terms of his leadership. Describe how his actions and follow-up would affect you as an alumnus of the institution and as a public citizen of this country.

2. Was the commandant being individually considerate to the cadets or merely observing the letter of the law? Would you have done anything differently? Why?

3. Was there sufficiently active managing by exception to control such occurrences? How much were the cadets at fault? Did initial cadet orientation fail?

4. Did the commandant enhance his idealized influence with the alumni?

5. What actions should the commandant take next on these issues?

CHAPTER

27

Jack Gets a Grip*

Jack Hartnett, president of D.L. Rogers Corporation, has expanded his Sonic restaurants franchise business to 51 units using management methods that even New Agers might find strange. His brand of fun and management involves tactics as leisurely as a staff picnic, or as hard-nosed as firing a manager for telling a lie. Hartnett says some might perceive his style of leadership as unorthodox, but no one can question his numbers. Fiscal 1995 sales for Sonic drive-ins have been estimated at more than $31 million, the highest of any franchisee in a chain that has 1,550 units in 27 Southern states. Much of the success of Hartnett's managerial model has to do with company openness. Hartnett is known as ruthlessly honest, and he expects the same from the ranks. To this end, he instituted Internal Health Surveys, questionnaires given intermittently to managers with hot-button fill-ins such as, "My supervisor's three worst traits." In addition, Hartnett insists on personal involvement among managers and supervisors, their families, and the head office.

Sonic operator Jack Hartnett has a controversial hold on his managers—but they're not complaining about the payback.

It's 4 A.M. You're sitting blindfolded in the back of a van trundling into the Missouri wilderness as music from *The Phantom of the Opera* blares from the cassette deck. After this jarring ride, you find yourself at a camp site. Your next several hours will be spent in the woods where, with the help of clue sheets and warnings about snakes and bears, you and your teammates will have to find ribbons faster than the opposing team can. But you won't win unless you return to camp playing kazoos.

---

*Klara, R. (1996). Jack gets a grip. *Restaurant Business, 95*(15), 38–48. (Adapted)

Welcome to a supervisors' meeting of the D.L. Rogers Corporation, part of the managerial play book of president Jack Hartnett, an outspoken yet exceedingly polite 44-year-old Texan who's expanded his Sonic franchise business to 51 units using management methods even New Agers might find strange.

The trek through the woods typifies the "lock-in," an intensive meeting often held in a surprise, no-escape location. Object: to build teamwork and "put the fun back into management," explains Hartnett. His brand of fun and management involves tactics as leisurely as a staff picnic, or as hard-nosed as firing a manager for telling a lie. "Some might perceive my style of leadership as unorthodox," he says, "But no one can question my numbers."

With the Bedford, TX-based company's 12 straight years of record profits, no one is likely to. "They have some of the highest profits in the chain," says Sonic marketing VP Pattye Moore. Hartnett won't get into specific figures, but fiscal '95 sales for D.L. Rogers' Sonic drive-ins have been estimated at well over $31 million, the highest of any franchisee in a chain that has 1,550 units in 27 Southern states. Hartnett says simply, "We're kicking everybody's tail."

If that sounds over-confident, Hartnett is unfazed. He's been in the restaurant industry since he was in junior high, and knows well enough what doesn't work. "I saw things I didn't like," Hartnett says of his ill-paid early days in fast food. "Honesty wasn't rewarded, the owner was unapproachable, there was no fairness." It was early on that what Hartnett calls the "I would have's" began. Seeing one supervisor lambaste an employee for offering criticism, he internalized the things he would have done differently in the same situation. "I wanted to create an environment," he says, "based on truth."

His chance would come soon enough. While Hartnett first came to Sonic as a manager trainee in 1976, D.L. Rogers founder and namesake Don L. Rogers made him director of operations in 1983 after luring him back from a stint as general manager of the Steinmann Corporation, an operator of nightclubs in the Houston area.

On his return, Hartnett saw the company as "a very splintered organization. There was no communication, no authority." He likens his reorganization to "getting control of a raging fire."

Much of the success of his managerial model has to do with company openness. "I'm known as ruthlessly honest," Hartnett says. He expects the same from the ranks. To this end, he instituted Internal Health Surveys, questionnaires given intermittently to managers with hot-button fill-ins like "My supervisor's three worst traits" and Yes/No's like "My supervisor manages me through intimidation." To assure candor, nobody has to sign his [or her] name. Similar surveys are also given to front-liners. "Then we go to the manager," Hartnett says with frank enthusiasm, "and say 'Here's what

your employee said about [your] restaurant. How can we work on this?' "
D.L. Rogers' no-secrets atmosphere springs from Hartnett's eight rules, a
sort of 10 commandments for restaurant operations. Admittedly, some can
seem Biblical in their seriousness. The first two ("I don't lie to you," "You
don't lie to me") are the foundation of Hartnett's corporate culture and not
to be taken lightly. "It has to do with the ethics of this business. We don't
build a company on mistrust," he says. "If you were late because you overslept, you'd better tell me you overslept. If I find out you lied, I'm going to
fire you."

Similarly, rule number eight—"I will only tell you one time"—allows little
room for unwillingness to correct mistakes. "The first [mistake] is ignorance," Hartnett says. "The second time is from a willingness to not do the
job."

For employees willing to work under such standards, the returns can
be significant. The average store manager in the D.L. Rogers Corporation
took home $65,000 last year; three out of his eight area supervisors made
$150,000. Managers also enjoy a 15% bonus plan, 100% health coverage, and
the chance to buy a 1% interest in other stores after three years. Hartnett's
own compensation includes loyalty: The average managerial tenure is over
nine years.

The proving ground for that loyalty is Hartnett's insistence on personal
involvement among managers and supervisors, their families, and the head
office. Regular phone calls and visits among managers and supervisors are
expected, and visits at home are not unusual. Even combined vacations are
encouraged. Perhaps most surprisingly, Hartnett's engagement in managers' personal problems is commonplace. "We get very involved in these
lives," he says. At various times, Hartnett has interceded in managers' personal finances ("If they can't handle their own money, they can't handle
mine," he says) and even in their marital problems.

That troubles Kristin Anderson, principal with Performance Research Associates, a Minneapolis-based management consulting firm. "A manager
and owner's job is not to be a parent figure or a psychologist, nor is it to
erase that line between work and home." She goes on to liken Hartnett's
managers joining the company to joining a church. But for those in the Rogers camp, the blurring of boundaries between personal and professional
lives has had recognizable benefits. "I can't tell you how many people are
still with us because Jack knew what the problem was, [and] we were able
to help them overcome it," says Oklahoma area supervisor Jim Simons. "It's
not that Jack tries to intrude on private life. I think he's genuinely interested
that things are going okay at home."

"Jack has never gotten into my personal finances without an invitation,"
says Michael Lewis, a manager in Oklahoma City, "I'll call him and say 'Jack,
I've got problems' [and] I felt better once I had talked with him about it."

Andy Rhue, manager of the Tyler, TX, Sonic observes: "To me, if the CEO calls me at home, I say 'He cares.' " Of course, Hartnett's reasons for caring go beyond altruism. The Sonic units of D.L. Rogers are limited liability companies based on shared ownership. A "manager/partner" typically owns a 25% stake, with 5% belonging to the area supervisor and the balance to Rogers. With compensation resting solely on unit dividends, "It's in our interest to make sure those managers are profitable, and that they make a good living," Simons says.

That effort extends to managers' personal lives because Hartnett believes troubles at home can quickly become company issues. "A [manager's] tax problem is really none of our business, but it is when it affects how he runs his store," says Simon.

Such financial scrutiny, however, seems secondary to what Hartnett and his managers describe as the overriding family atmosphere in the company. Simons envisions management in other restaurant outfits as "cutthroat situations [where] everyone's trying to up the other guy. But [here]," he says, "with the other supervisors I'd do anything in the world to help them." When Hartnett opens a new Sonic, he'll typically rent a house nearby and invite up to 20 managers to live there together while the new unit's operations are polished. For Hartnett, it's an opportunity to cement relationships and do some cooking. For managers like Lewis, it's a chance to pick some brains. "I usually try to bring back 10 new ideas each time I go."

But for some, Hartnett's brand of team work is too intense. Recently D.L. Rogers' top-netting manager left the company, literally, by packing his bags in the middle of the night during a store opening. "It sent a huge, bad message to the rest of the group," Hartnett says. It is also a reminder that tactics like Hartnett's, however successful, don't have universal appeal. They rate high in what's become known in the training field as the "woo woo factor," which is used to describe out-in-the-woods scenarios replacing in-office training techniques. "A lot of people are doing those kinds of things," observes Ron Zemke, Performance Research Associates' president, "but there's not much data that says it's better or worse than anything else."

The World According to Jack

"The president of a company renting a house, putting his directors in a van, blindfolded, and making them listen to tapes, that's a very different [approach]," admits Sonic's Moore. "Jack doesn't do business the way most managers do, [but] there's no disputing that it works. In fact, I've contemplated doing some of his techniques myself." If she decides to, she'll have to be willing to spend $190,000 to bring 234 people (managers, supervisors, and families) to Cancun, Mexico, which is what Hartnett did this past July for D.L. Rogers' biennial convention. This year's four-day gathering featured supervisors and their spouses dressed like tribal warriors and ancient Egyptians.

But the events, in true company form, mixed clowning with education. Employees attended seminars with titles like "Epoch Mythology" and "Sand Skirmish" which were actually brass tacks classes about time management and teamwork. And in true Hartnett form, they also blended business with home life. The "Romancing the Stone" program featured tips on being a better spouse.

For a manager like Michael Lewis, the seminars are the only cure for "store blindness," which sets in when the 65–75-per-week on-site hours dull his senses. "When I come back from a convention," he says, "I come back with an attitude change. It's about improving me, because by improving me my store improves."

Lewis tracks about 750 people through his Sonic every day, and his $75,000 in monthly sales are a good return for an event that seems no more complicated than a family reunion.

Nonetheless, Hartnett's management model thrives only because his people, although franchisees, act as independent operators. "You can't do some of the things we do if [managers] were employees," he says. "You can if they're partners." Zemke concurs. "The idea of being partnered with your managers is a really good idea," he says, "[but] it would be awfully hard to have policies and procedures like his in a large company." He calls Hartnett an entrepreneur whose methods, while "powerful stuff," are "limited to the entrepreneurial venture."

"Entrepreneur" is one way to describe Jack Hartnett. The managers who presented him with a plaque which currently hangs in his office have another. "Thank you for your time and your effort," it reads. "Presented to our mother superior."

Discussion Questions

1. What are some of the drawbacks to Harnett's style?
2. Do you think his style would work in a larger corporation?
3. How would you coach Harnett to improve his style of leadership?
4. Do you think his style is ethical?
5. How do you think female followers would react to his style compared with male followers?

28

The Fine Art of Leadership*

In an interview, James Burke, former chairman and CEO of Johnson & Johnson (J&J) and current chairman of the Partnership for a Drug-Free America and The Business Enterprise Trust (BET), discussed the drive to eradicate illegal drugs in America and the fostering of corporate ethics and social responsibility. Burke believes there are three big problems in America today: illegal drugs, the educational system, and the breakdown of the family. He discussed what CEOs and their businesses can do to shape personal ethics and social policies in their communities.

The name *James Burke* belongs in the highest echelon of leadership and corporate ethics.

One of the most respected senior executives in America, Burke was chairman and CEO of Johnson & Johnson in 1982 when seven people died from ingesting Tylenol Extra-Strength capsules that had been laced with cyanide. (The culprit has never been caught.) Burke's decisive leadership included absolute honesty with the media, an executive team devoted full time to the situation, and the unprecedented step of removing every bottle of Tylenol from sale during the crisis. Because J&J had a solid reputation as a company responsive to its consumers, it weathered the calamity as well as another poisoning incident in 1986. The Tylenol saga became a crisis-management legend and the stuff of business school textbook case studies.

Burke retired from J&J in 1989, and became chairman of the Partnership for a Drug-Free America and The Business Enterprise Trust (BET), two asso-

---

*Ettore, B., & Burke, J. (1996). The Fine Art of Leadership. *Management Review, 85*(10), 13–16. (Adapted)

ciations committed to high-profile issues: eradicating illegal drugs in America and fostering corporate ethics and social responsibility.

Q. People immediately single out the . . . Tylenol crisis as the paradigm of corporate ethical behavior and are hard-pressed to come up with a more recent example. What does this say about the state of American business ethics?

Burke: Well, a lot of things. One of the things it suggests is that it was one of the most dramatic incidents in history, and it will always stand that way. I don't think anybody's going to come up with one more dramatic. The fact is, all of a sudden, seven people died, and our product was the instrument of their death. It was a product that had a tremendous safety profile, and a company that everybody trusted.

Q. Did you take it personally?

Burke: No. Now, I think the reason I was successful—and I did a very good job, by the way—was the reputation of the corporation. There's no question about that in my mind. The company had always behaved well with its constituencies—incidentally, because they were in the baby [product] business and the Band-Aid business, which is close to everybody's heart. It caused people to think in terms of children and the word "trust." Everybody trusted us. So, when I went before the public and said, "Trust us," they did.

I did not think we would be as successful as we were, but I knew from the beginning that we were not going to lose the business. I thought we'd lose about 30 percent of our market share and never get it back. We had a much bigger business than we would have had without the [crisis], as it turned out. It was so dramatic—it led the news every single night on every station for six weeks. I mean, it was relentless. The media turned out to be on our side.

Q. Can you elaborate?

Burke: I went to the media. After this happened, I called the chairman of each network and told them I wanted to talk to the head of news, but I didn't want them there, and I didn't want anyone else there. And I wasn't going to bring anybody. I talked to the head of news at each network, alone. There was no public relations spiel. I said, "I want you to know we're going to give you all the information we have. We're going to play it straight with you. At the moment, we don't have any poison in our plants that could account for this, but we're doing a lot of investigating, and I will keep you informed." And we found that we did.

Q.   Everyone left the minions outside? That's very unusual.

Burke: It's one of the reasons I did it. I wanted them to trust me, and I wanted them to know that I trusted them. Most Americans could buy any product at any time, anywhere, with complete safety. Now, all of a sudden, that was challenged, and they could be in a position of mistrusting everything. I said, "That is a very serious public health and safety problem."

Q.   Did the fact that you put it on the line with them in terms of "I will be there, too" help?

Burke: Yes. Furthermore, I went to the head of the FBI, Bill Webster. I told him what I thought we ought to do. It was his opinion that there was an overreaction, the removal of all the products. I hadn't completely persuaded him, but he said, "This is your call": I then went to the FDA. They didn't want me to [remove the products] either. I said, "I think you're going to get copycat cases anyway. If you don't act aggressively, you're going to have more than if you do." In the middle of that conversation, the head of the FDA was called out. I sat there for 15 or 20 minutes. He came back in and said, "Guess what? You're right. We've got a copycat in California."
           Once that happened, I told the media heads, "I've talked to the head of the FDA. I've talked to the head of the FBI. Both are ready to talk to you at your convenience, and you have an open line to them. They're going to tell it the way they see it. I'm going to tell it the way I see it. Your responsibility is well beyond telling the news, it's to help the public get through this."

Q.   Isn't this exemplary CEO behavior?

Burke: Yes. But I think it's rooted in something. I was lucky. I had a family who thought the same way. The company I went to work for thought [the same way].

Q.   It is not generally known that Daniel Burke [well regarded retired president of Capital Cities] is your brother.

Burke: I have a sister, Phyllis, who is a [retired] group vice president of Avon and another sister, Sydney, who was a lawyer. She had five children and went to law school while she had them.

Q. What kind of family gave rise to these accomplished children?

Burke: It's interesting. We grew up in a small town. Whatever that afforded us, I think it was considerable. I think our mother and father were both remarkable. My father didn't see too many gray areas. He was Catholic. He really wasn't very tolerant of immorality. If he had an intolerance, that was it. He also was a very warm, outgoing, tough man.

Q. What did he do for a living?

Burke: He started as a salesman in a marble company in Vermont, then ended up as a life insurance salesman. He also was the youngest field major in the Army in World War I. He chose to be a second lieutenant in the regular Army rather than a first lieutenant in the reserves. In the field they made him a major at a very young age, 22.

Q. Did he earn any decorations?

Burke: Yes, he did. He won them later. So, he was a remarkable model. My mother, on the other hand, was intellectual, very creative, and loved contention.

Q. So the dinner table probably saw some heated discussions.

Burke: That's it. My father would usually get up after a while, [then] walk [out] and read the paper. But the rest of us knew that when we arrived at the table, we'd better be *au courant* about what was going on in the world because we didn't know what we were going to have to discuss. We argued all the time—still do. That was a great educational process for all of us.

Q. Did your mother work outside the home?

Burke: She didn't, but secretly wished she had. She was a genuine feminist in every bone in her body. We were brought up to believe that women and men were the same as far as opportunity was concerned. We had to go out in the real world before we realized that was not quite true.

Q.   Was modesty part of your family's ethic?

Burke: I don't think I'm modest.

Burke's leadership style: "I have tried to recreate the climate that I had in my own home. I love to stimulate people to argue with each other and to feel that that's what they're here for—that it is a creative process. People think that when they're all talking at once, it bothers me.

Discussion Questions

1. Would Burke have the same attitudes toward morality in business if he were CEO of a company not involved with health and babies?
2. What are the key strengths of Burke's style of leadership?
3. Why don't other leaders act in as moralistic a way as Burke seems to act?
4. How important to Burke's moral stance was his family?
5. Can we develop the type of leadership that Burke displays? If so, then how?

Author Index

A

Aburdene, Patricia, 43
Atwater, L. E., 8, *10*
Avolio, B. J., 5, 7, 8, *10*

B

Bass, B. M., 5, 7, 8, *10*
Berger, S., 84
Burke, J., 164
Business Week, 29, 59
Butler, C., 24

C

Camobreco, J., 8, *10*
Churchill, N. C., 98
Cohen, E. A., 73
Crosby, R., 57

D

Donlon, J. P., 138

E

Einstein, W. O., 5, *10*
Enderle, G., 149
Ettore, B., 164

F

Financial World, 29

G

Government Executive, 40

H

Hater, J. J., 5, *10*
Higgins, C. A., 5, *10*
House, R. J., 8, *10*
Howell, J. M., 5, 8, *10*

I

Inc., 44

J

Johnson, G., 36
Johnson, N., 36

K

Kaplan, J., 79
Katz, A. J., 20
Klara, R., 159
Kleiner, B. H., 96
Kroeck, K. G., 6, *10*

L

Lau, A. W., 8, *10*
Leithwood, K., 5, *10*
Levinson, H., 2, *10*
Lienert, A., 48
Lowe, K., 6, *10*

M

McClelland, D. C., 8, *10*
McClenahen, J. S., 76
Murphy, P., 149

N

New Management Magazine, 90

O

Olberding, S., 55
Onnen, M. K., 5, *10*

S

Salter, D. J., 5, *10*
Shamir, B., 1, *10*
Sivasubramaniam, N., 6, *10*
Starr, Jennifer, 45
Steinbach, R., 5, *10*

T

Tapsell, S., 62
Tower, W., 98
Tropilla, D., 96

U

Upbin, B., 77

W

Wachs, E., 42, 46
Waldman, D. A., 5, *10*
Whitmore, N., 8, *10*
Willamette Week, 38
Winston, M. G., 88
Wolf, W., 98

Y

Yammarino, F. J., 5, *10*

Subject Index

A

Accountability, *see* Single-point accountability
Active management by exception, 4
Advertising, at Columbia Sportswear, 81–82
Aerospace industry, *see* AlliedSignal Corporation
Age of Reason (Paine), 9
Airborne Express, 45
Airline industry, *see* Southwest Airlines
ALCOA, *see* Aluminum Company of America
Allen, Robert, 80
AlliedSignal Corporation, 24, 28–29, 76–78
Aluminum Company of America (ALCOA), 55–61
Amerman, John, 138
Andersen Consulting, 32
Anderson, Kristin, 161
Apple Computer, Inc., 79, 89
Appraisal, *see* Assessment
Ash, Mary Kay, 24, 25–26
Ash, Stephen, 25
Assessment, of employees, 76–77
AT&T, 80
Authoritarian leadership, 6–7
　　Don Simonic at ALCOA, 55, 56, 57–61
　　Walter Tower at Nimrod Press, 99
Automobile industry
　　Nancy Badore of Ford, 96, 97
　　Chrysler Corporation, 48–53, 79
　　corporate cultures, 50
　　Robert Eaton, 48–53
　　in Europe, 51

General Motors and General Motors Europe, 48–49, 50, 52
　　Japanese management, 51–52
　　Mexico and, 52–53
　　women and minorities in, 53
Automotive parts industry
　　AlliedSignal, 24, 28–29
　　Springfield Remanufacturing Corporation, 24, 27–28
Autonomous work teams, 57, see also Team-based management
Avon, 142, 167

B

Badore, Nancy, 96, 97
Baltimore Colts, 56
BankAmerica, 140
Barad, Jill Elikann, 138–146
Barad, Tom, 140
Barbie, 138, 139, 142, 143, 144
Beard, Daniel, 40
Ben and Jerry's, 14
Best Boss/Worst Boss Contest, 33
Bianco, Don, 33
Bismarck, Otto von, 7
Blank, Arthur, 32
Bonuses, 122
Borders, Perrin & Norrander ad agency, 81
Bosch, Robert, 78
Bossidy, Lawrence, 24, 28–29, 76–78
Boyle, Gertrude, 70, 79, 81–83
Boyle, Neal, 81
Boyle, Tim, 81

Brands, 142–143
Bribes, 150
British senior service, 41
Brown, Gary, 27
Buck, Vicki, 62, 64–65
Bureau of Reclamation, U.S., 40
Burke, Daniel, 166
Business Enterprise Trust, 164–165
Business ethics, 147, *see also* Ethical
  management
  James Burke, 164–168
  Adrian Cadbury, 149–150

C

Cadbury, George Adrian, 149–150
Cadbury Commission, 150
Cadbury Schweppes, 149–150
Cadres, 60
Catalyst leadership, 40
Catholic Health Corporation, 84–86
CDW, 45
Cellular technology, at Motorola, 89, 94
Chamberlain, Winston, 101
Change management, *see also* Strategic
  change
  communication and, 77
  ˋemployee appraisal, 76–77
  renewal concept at Motorola, 88–95
  Don Simonic at ALCOA, 55–61
Charity, 30
Child-care benefits, 30, 31
Children's clothing industry, *see* Hanna
  Andersson
Christchurch (New Zealand), 64–65
Christman, Daniel W., 154–157
Chrysler Corporation, 79
  Robert Eaton, 48–53
Clancy, J. Anthony, 32
Clothing industry
  Columbia Sportswear, 79, 80, 81–83
  Hanna Andersson, 24, 30–31
Cocchiola, Michael J., 39, 40
Collaborative management, *see also*
  Communication
  catalyst role, 40
  by government executives, 36–41
  leadership qualities, 41

David Leclaire on, 36
  Gov. Roberts of Oregon, 36, 37–38
Columbia Sportswear, 79, 80, 81–83
Command and control management, 36
Commercial/financial printing industry,
  see Printing industry
Common Sense (Paine), 9
Communication/communication systems,
  119, *see also* Collaborative man-
  agement; Listening
  in change management, 77
  enterprise resource planning, 130–132
  at PC Connection, 45–46
Community change, 64–65
Community colleges, 20–23
Community partnerships, 23
Community service, 85–86
Computer chip industry, 89
Computer industry
  microprocessors, 89
  PC Connection, 42–46
Consideration, 67, 68
Constructive transaction, 4, 6, 122, *see also*
  Contingent reward;
  Transactional leadership
Consultative decision-making, 60
Consumer brand companies, 139, 142
Contingent reward, 1, 3, 4, 122, *see also*
  Constructive transaction;
  Transactional leadership
"Conversation with Oregon," 36, 37–38
Corporate Coach, The (Miller), 33
Corporate culture
  American automobile industry, 50
  opposition to change and innovation,
  134–136
Corrective leadership, 1–2, 68, *see also*
  Transactional leadership
Cosmetics industry, 140
  Avon, 142, 167
  Mary Kay Cosmetics, 24, 25–26
Coty Cosmetics, 140
Counter-intuitive thinking, 93–94
Credibility, 152–153
Crosby, Patricia and Robert, 56, 57–58, 60
"Customer First" strategy, 113–114
Customer relations
  Home Depot, 32–33
  Southwest Airlines, 13–14

D

D. L. Rogers Corporation, 159–163
Database systems, enterprise resource
    planning, 130–132
Defense Printing Service, 39
Democratic leadership, 6
Denhart, Gun, 24, 30–31
Denhart, Tom, 30
Directive leadership, 6–7
Direct mail industry, see Mail-order industry
Discretion, in management, 66
Disney, see Walt Disney Company
Drucker, Peter, 127
Dunn, Arthur, 25, 33–34

E

Eastern Airlines, 13
Eaton, Robert J., 48–53
Emerson, Hank, 74–75
Employee assessment, 76–77
Employee benefits
    Hanna Anderson, 30, 31
    Home Depot, 32
    Mattel, 145
Employee management/relations
    collaborative leadership and, 39
    Columbia Sportswear, 82
    Hanna Anderson, 30–31
    Home Depot, 32–33
    Mary Kay Cosmetics, 25–26
    Mattel, 145
    MCQ Associates, 35
    Motorola, 34, 90
    PC Connection, 45–46
    Sonic restaurants, 160–163
    Southwest Airlines, 14
Employee motivation, see also Inspirational
    leadership/motivation
    at Hanna Anderson, 31
Employee training
    AlliedSignal, 29
    Home Depot, 32
    Springfield Manufacturing Corp., 27–28
Empowerment, 39, see also Team-based
    management
    at ALCOA, 57
    Colin Powell on, 17

Energy Department, U.S., 39
Enterprise Group, 22
Enterprise resource planning (ERP),
    130–132
Entrepreneurs, Walter Tower on, 98, 99
ERP, see Enterprise resource planning
Ethical management, see also Moral
    principles
    James Burke, 164–168
    Adrian Cadbury, 149–150
    credibility and, 152–153
    Jack Hartnett, 160–161
    Tylenol crisis, 164, 165–166
    West Point marriage case, 154–157
Europe
    government-industry relationship, 51
    Mattel, 142
Executive development, 96, 97

F

Fairness
    Adrian Cadbury's management style,
    149, 150
    Jack Hartnett's management style,
    160–161
Family businesses
    leadership transition at Columbia
    Sportswear, 79, 80, 81–83
    leadership transition at Nimrod Press,
    98–106
Family life, see also Work-life balance
    Jack Hartnett's management style
    and, 161–162
FBI, see Federal Bureau of Investigation
FDA, see Food and Drug Administration
Federal Bureau of Investigation (FBI), 166
Federal officials, see Government
    executives
Feedback
    four-directional (360°), 93, 135–136
    meetings, 119
Female leaders, see Women
Financial training, 27–28
Fisher-Price, 141
Flanigen, Debra, 35
Food and Drug Administration (FDA), 166
Ford Motor Company, 96, 97
Four-directional feedback, 93, 135–136

Four Is, 4–5, *see also* Idealized leadership/influence; Individualized concern; Inspirational leadership/motivation; Intellectual stimulation
Full range leadership model
    elements of, 3
    optimal and sub-optimal profiles of, 4–5
    research findings on, 5
Full Range of Leadership Development Program, 8
Fun, *see* Humor

G

Gallup, Patricia, 42–46
Galvin, Bob, 90, 94
Galvin, Chris, 90
Galvin, Paul, 89, 90, 93–94
GAP reviews, 125–126
General Electric Company, 76
General Foods, 142
General managers, project development and, 127–129
General Motors, 48–49, 50
General Motors Europe, 48, 49, 50, 52
Gerstner, Louis, 79, 80–81
Gharajedaghi, Jamshid, 21
Gifts, 150
Gillette, 139
Goals, 122
    strategic change and, 117–118
Government executives, *see also* Public leaders
    collaborative management, 36–41
Governors, Barbara Roberts, 36, 37–38
Greenwald, Gerald, 79
Gregor, Joie, 80
Grogan, Barbara, 96–97
Grotte, Helena, 30, 31
Growney, Bob, 90

H

Hall, David, 42, 43, 44, 45
Hanna Andersson, 24, 30–31
Hannadown Program, 30
Hartnett, Jack, 159–163
Hasbro, 139

Heagy, Linda, 80
Healthcare Forum, 84, 85, 86–87
Healthcare industry
    Catholic Health Corporation, 84–86
    Healthcare Forum, 84, 85, 86–87
    leadership development, 84, 85, 86–87
Heidrick & Struggles, 80
Hitler, Adolf, 8, 9
Home Depot, 24, 32–33
Honesty, Jack Hartnett's management style and, 160–161
Hot Wheels, 142, 144
Howser, Lee, 20–23
Humor, 124
    Jill Barad, 145
    Vicki Buck, 64
    Colin Powell, 74
    Southwest Airlines, 14

I

Iacocca, Lee A., 48, 49–50
IBM, 79, 80–81, 89
Idealized leadership/influence, 2, 4, 5, 67
Individualized concern, 3, 5, 7, 67, 118–120
Individualized development, 39
Industrial accidents, 55, 56
Initiation, 67, 68
Innovation, Motorola's concept of renewal, 88–95
Inspirational leadership/motivation, 2, 4, 5, 7, 67, 120–121
Integrated information technology, 130, 131, *see also* Enterprise resource planning
Integrated performance leadership system, 93
Intel, 89
Intellectual stimulation, 2–3, 4, 7, 67, 121–122
Internal facilitators, 57, 59
Internal Health Surveys, 159, 160
Internal value systems, 113
Iridium project (Motorola, Inc.), 91

J

Jackson Area Quality Initiative, 23
Jackson Community College, 20–23

Jackson Community Transformation
    Project, 23
Japan
    government-industry relationship, 51
    management style, 51–52
    Mattel, 142
Jefferson, Thomas, 16
Johnson & Johnson, 164, 165–166

K

Kelleher, Herb, 13–14
Kincaid, Don, 45
Knight, Phil, 83
Krasny, Michael, 45

L

Laissez-faire leadership, 2, 4, 6, 68–69,
    see also Passive leadership
Laughter and leadership, see Humor
Leadership development, in the healthcare
    industry, 84, 85, 86–87
Leadership of renewal, Motorola, 88–95
Leadership transition
    Chrysler, 49–50
    Columbia Sportswear, 79, 80, 81–83
    Nimrod Press, 98, 99–106
Learning organizations, 23
Leclaire, David, 36, 39
"Legacy-leaving," 91–92
Letarte, Clyde, 21
Lewis, Michael, 161, 162, 163
Lienert, Anita Pyzik, 49
Limperis, Jim, 34
Listening
    in change management, 77
    in collaborative management, 36–41
Love Cosmetics, 140
Loyalty
    Jack Hartnett's management style, 161
    Motorola, 92
Lytle, Jill, 39

M

Mail-order industry
    Hanna Andersson, 30–31
    PC Connection, 42–46

Management authority, Don Simonic at
    ALCOA, 55, 56, 57–61
Management by exception, 1–2, 4, 123–124
Management retreats, 134–136
Management training, 96, 97
Marcus, Bernard, 24, 32–33
Marine Corps commanders, 5
Market windows, strategic change and,
    112–114, 127
Mary Kay Cosmetics, 24, 25–26
Matchbox, 141, 142, 144
Mattel, 138–146
Maturity, healthcare leaders and, 85
Max Factor, 140
Mayors
    Vicki Buck, 62, 64–65
    Fran Wilde, 63
McCombs, Tom, 55, 56, 57, 58, 59–61
MCQ Associates, 25, 34–35
McQiddy, John, 25, 34–35
Measure 5 (Oregon), 37–38
Media, Tylenol crisis and, 164, 165–166
Megatrends for Women (Aburdene), 43
Methodist ministers, 5
Mexico, Chrysler and, 52–53
Microprocessor industry, 89
Microsoft, 46, 140
Milhoan, James, 40
Military leaders/leadership
    Colin Powell, 18, 73, 74–75
    transformational leadership and, 5
    West Point marriage case, 154–157
Miller, Jim, 33
Millwriting companies, 96–97
Minard, Randall, 45
Ministers, 5
Minorities
    automobile industry and, 53
    racial discrimination, 73
    toy marketing and, 143
"Minority reports," 94
Mission-critical networks, strategic change
    and, 112–114
MLQ, see Multifactor Leadership
    Questionnaire
Moeller, A. Diane, 84–87
Moore, Demi, 139
Moore, Pattye, 160, 162

Moral principles, 8–9, *see also* Ethical management
Motivation, *see* Employee motivation; Inspirational leadership/ motivation
Motorola, Inc.
   company performance, 88–89
   Arthur Dunn of Motorola Information Systems, 25, 33–34
   future prospects, 94–95
   institutional heritage, 89–90
   Iridium project, 91
   leadership of renewal principle, 90–92
   legacy concept, 91
   "minority reports," 94
   renewal of leadership principle, 92–93
   thinking the unthinkable principle, 93–94
Multifactor Leadership Questionnaire (MLQ), 2
My American Journey (Powell), 16, 74

N

NAFTA, *see* North American Free Trade Agreement
NASA, *see* National Aeronautics and Space Administration
National Aeronautics and Space Administration (NASA), 39, 40
Naval officers, 5
NEC, 89
Netscape, 46
Networking, in healthcare leadership development, 86
New Zealand
   Vicki Buck, 62, 64–65
   Fran Wilde, 62–64
Nike, 83
Nimrod Press
   company background, 98–99
   succession issue, 99–101
   Walter Tower's management style, 99
   transition of leadership, 102–106
No-marriage policy, West Point Military Academy, 154–157
North American Free Trade Agreement (NAFTA), 53
Nuclear Regulatory Commission, 40

O

O'Neill, Paul, 56
Openness
   Adrian Cadbury's management style, 149, 150
   Jack Hartnett's management style, 160–161
Open plan organization, 63–64
Open systems, 56, *see also* Team-based management
Oregon, 36, 37–38
Organizational culture, *see* Corporate culture
Organizational restructuring
   Jill Barad at Mattel, 138–146
   enterprise resource planning and, 130–132
Outdoor clothing industry, *see* Columbia Sportswear
Overseas operating experience, 52

P

Paine, Thomas, 9
Palisin, Ernie, 32–33
Participative leadership, 6
Partnership for a Drug-Free America, 164–165
Passive leadership, 121, *see also* Laissez-faire leadership
Passive management by exception, 4
PC Connection, 42–46
Pension Benefit Guaranty Corporation, 38
PepsiCo, 79
Performance Research Associates, 161, 162
Personalized leadership, 8, 9
Peterson, Malcolm, 40
Pixar, 140
Political leaders, *see* Public leaders
Positive reinforcement, 26
Powell, Colin L.
   background, 73
   comments on leadership, 16–19
   qualities of leadership in, 73–75
Pregnancy policy, West Point Military Academy, 156–157
Printing industry

Defense Printing Service, 39
  Nimrod Press, 98–106
Proctor & Gamble, 56, 139, 142
Product development, strategic change
  and, 113–114, 126–128
Project teams, 127–129
Pseudo leaders, 152–153
  pseudotransactional, 9
  pseudotransformational, 8, 9, 67–68
Public leaders, see also Government
  executives
  Vicki Buck, 62, 64–65
  Barbara Roberts, 36, 37–38
  Fran Wilde, 62–63

Q

Quality management, 21
  AlliedSignal, 29

R

R. R. Donnelley & Sons, 80
Racial discrimination, 73
RCA, 93
Reciprocal loyalty, 92
Reengineering, see Organizational
  restructuring
Renewal concept, 88–95, see also
  Self-renewal
Research and development
  MCQ Associates, 25, 34–35
  strategic change and, 125–129
Restaurant industry, see Hartnett, Jack;
  Sonic restaurants
Rhue, Andy, 162
Right side-left side activity, 22–23
Rights of Man (Paine), 9
RJR Nabisco, 79
Roberts, Barbara, 36, 37–38
Rogers, Don L., 160
Roosevelt, Eleanor, 8
Rotation of managers, 91–92

S

School principals, 5
Schwinn, Carole, 21, 23
Sculley, John, 79
Security, healthcare leaders and, 85

Self-confidence, 74
Self-directed work teams, 57, see also
  Team-based management
Self-renewal, 92
Seminar (Mary Kay Cosmetics), 26
Senge, Peter, 22, 23
Service, see Community service
Sexual stereotyping, 144
Simonic, Don, 55, 56, 57–58, 59, 60, 61
Simons, Jim, 161, 162
Single-point accountability, 58–59
Smith, Jack, 50
Social change, 64–65
Socialized leadership, 8–9
Sonic restaurants, 159–163
Southwest Airlines, 13–14
Spear, Arthur, 140
Springfield Remanufacturing Corporation,
  24, 27–28
Stack, Jack, 24, 27–28
Stalin, Joseph, 8, 9
Stein, Bruce, 139
Steinmann Corporation, 160
Step review process, 125–126, 128
Stereotyping, sexual, 144
Stock options
  Home Depot, 32
  PC Connection, 46
Strategic business units (SBUs), 126
Strategic change/planning
  Jill Barad at Mattel, 138–146
  Catholic Health Corporation, 85–86
  collaborative management and, 40
  enterprise resource planning and,
    130–132
  example interview with division
    manager regarding, 116–124
  example memos outlining, 111–114,
    125–129
  organizational opposition to, 134–136
Succession, see also Leadership transition
  at Nimrod Press, 99–101
Sun Microsystems, 14
SWOT analysis, 63

T

Team-based management
  at ALCOA, 56, 57, 58, 59, 60–61

consultative decision-making and, 60
Arthur Dunn at Motorola, 34
Robert Eaton on, 49
Team resource, 57, *see also* Internal
    facilitators
Teamwork, in healthcare leadership
    development, 86
Technology management, Motorola's
    concept of renewal, 88–95
Telecommunications industry,
    see Motorola, Inc.
360° feedback, 93, 135–136
Tooker, Gary, 90
Tour management, 66–67, 68
Tower, Caleb, 99, 100, 101
Tower, Ethan, 99–100
Tower, Joshua, 99
Tower, Seth, 98, 99, 100–106
Tower, Walter, 98–99, 100–106
Toy companies
    Hasbro, 139
    Mattel, 138–146
    Tyco Toys, 139, 140, 141, 144
Trade New Zealand, 62, 63–64
Tradenz, 62, 63–64
Transactional leadership, *see also*
        Constructive transaction;
        Contingent reward
    augmentation by transformational
    leadership, 1, 6, 68
    components of, 3–4
    corrective transactions, 68
    effectiveness of, 1–2
    qualities and characteristics of, viii, 1
Transformational leadership
    augmentation of transactional
    leadership, 1, 6, 68
    components of, 2–3, 67
    as democratic or authoritarian, 6–7
    effectiveness of, 1, 5–6
    personalized, 8, 9
    qualities and characteristics of, viii, 7–8
    research findings on, 5
    socialized, 8–9
Transition, *see* Leadership transition
Trust, Tylenol crisis and, 165
Tyco Toys, 139, 140, 141, 144
Tylenol crisis, 164, 165–166

U

United Airlines, 79
United Kingdom
    British senior service, 41
    ethical management of Adrian
    Cadbury, 149–150
U.S. Army, *see* Military leaders/leadership;
        West Point Military Academy
Utilitarianism, 8

V

Value systems, 113
Visionary leadership
    collaborative management and, 40
    Lee Howser, 20–23

W

W. K. Kellogg Foundation, 23
Walking the Empowerment Tightrope
    (Crosby), 57
Wall Street Journal (newspaper), 150
Walt Disney Company, 144–145
Walter, John, 80
Ward, Matt, 46
Washington, George, 16
Webster, William, 166
Welch, John F., Jr., 29, 76
Wellington (New Zealand), 63
Western Industrial Contractors, 96–97
West Point Military Academy, 154–157
WestWard Pay Strategies, 46
Wigbels, Lynn, 39
Wilde, Fran, 62–64
Women
    Mary Kay Ash, 24, 25–26
    automobile industry and, 53
    Nancy Badore, 96, 97
    Gertrude Boyle, 70, 79, 81–83
    Vicki Buck, 62, 64–65
    Gun Denhart, 24, 30–31
    future accessibility to leadership
    positions, 87
    Patricia Gallup, 42–46
    Barbara Grogan, 96–97
    A. Diane Moeller, 84–87
    Gov. Barbara Roberts, 36, 37–38

Fran Wilde, 62–64
Women Entrepreneurs (Starr), 45
Wood, Don, 28
Work flow processes, enterprise
    resource planning, 131
Work-life balance
  Nancy Badore of Ford Motor
  Company, 97
  Jill Barad at Mattel, 140, 145

Barbara Grogan at Western Industrial
  Contractors, 97
Workplaces, 51

Z

Zemke, Ron, 162, 163
Zenith, 93
Zock, Joe, 101

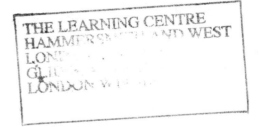